Levels of Schizophrenia

Levels of Schizophrenia

by
ALBERT E. SCHEFLEN, M.D.

BRUNNER/MAZEL, *Publishers* • New York

Library of Congress Cataloging in Publication Data

Scheflen, Albert E.
  Levels of schizophrenia.

  Includes bibliographies and index.
  1. Schizophrenia.   I. Title.   [DNLM: 1.   Schizophrenia.
  2. Social environment.   WM203 S317L]
  RC514.S319   616.89'82   80-21030
  ISBN 0-87630-252-5

Published by
BRUNNER/MAZEL, INC.
19 Union Square
New York, New York 10003

MANUFACTURED IN THE UNITED STATES OF AMERICA

About the Author

This book is the capstone to a life. Albert Scheflen devoted his life to schizophrenia and to fields peripheral to schizophrenia. For many years he had been a student of systems theory but he never found a way to apply this new way of thinking to schizophrenia. About five years ago he returned to the problem and began the complex task of trying to reconceptualize the separate fields of schizophrenia with systems theory. He was excited about the potential in the new effort. After he developed a lung cancer in the spring of 1979, he found the energy to record his new ideas as clearly as they could be stated in the light of present knowledge. This volume represents the final effort of a gifted researcher on the conceptual dilemma of schizophrenia.

As a thinker, Scheflen was far ahead of his time. He somehow had to know all there was to be known about every field that captured his interest. He became a fountainhead of knowledge about mental illness, psychiatric research, science, philosophy, and the various fields that dealt with human thinking and behavior. In addition to his extensiveness of knowledge, he had a rare gift in reducing complex knowledge into simple concepts. For instance, I probably learned more about general systems theory from a few meetings with Al in the mid-1960s than from weeks reading the original authors. The same applied to Gregory Bateson and epistemology. I learned more about epistemology from Scheflen than from years of association with Bateson. And so it went with every area of complex knowledge. Scheflen often referred to Aristotle who believed the understanding of complex material required that it be reduced to one main causal idea and perhaps one or two contributing ideas. In the reduction of complexity to simplicity something essential is lost. Then it is necessary to go back to the complex material and "boil it down" again, and to keep repeating the process to gain full understanding. This is the way Al Scheflen approached the complexity of schizophrenia. I hope the readers of this volume can be aware of the process in Scheflen as he tried to work toward a new way of thinking about schizophrenia.

Scheflen's first interest was neuropathology and neurophysiology. Then he shifted to psychiatry and psychoanalysis, at which he was an expert of experts. Then came the more peripheral fields of kinesics, communication, the family, and cultural and societal forces. Schizophrenia was always at the core of his life interests. His effort to conceptualize schizophrenia with systems concepts began after he read Gunderson's 1974 report, which Scheflen mentions in the preface to this book. That report was a thorough review of current research in schizophrenia. It covered many sciences and ended with doubts about anyone being able to put it all together. Scheflen was challenged by the Gunderson paper. He spent the next years rereading the neurosciences and numerous other basic writings. In the course of rereading and "boiling it down" there came the notion of eight separate levels of schizophrenia all interconnected within a systems framework. This is what this book is all about.

There was a memorable event in March 1977 in New York that may have contributed to Scheflen's systems thinking. Milton Berger organized the Beyond the Double Bind Conference that brought together a group which had been working with schizophrenia when the "double bind" concept was introduced in the 1950s by Bateson and the Palo Alto group. Participants included Bateson, Haley, Weakland, Bowen, Scheflen, Whitaker, and Wynne, and Margaret Mead who participated from the audience. Scheflen was active in the discussion of systems ideas as they had evolved the past 20 years.

Gregory Bateson developed an inoperable lung cancer in March 1978 for which he declined palliative therapy. He wanted to keep his mind clear to finish an important book. His cancer went into regression and he had a remarkably productive two years. He died in July 1980 of heart-lung problems not directly associated with cancer. Scheflen developed his inoperable lung cancer in March 1979. His way of dealing with it may have been patterned to some degree on Bateson's effort. His head was filled with vast knowledge about schizophrenia no one else possessed. There was a powerful motivation to record as much of it as possible and make it available to future generations. This volume is the result. Along the way he became interested in conceptualizing cancer as a multifaceted evolution in the life process rather than a pathology. His thinking about cancer sparkled with the same pattern that characterized his life. He died in August 1980 after this book had gone to press.

I first met Al shortly after I came east to NIMH for my family research in 1954. Our closest relationship began at the semi-annual meetings of the Group for the Advancement of Psychiatry in Asbury Park, New Jersey. I was attracted by his far-ranging thinking and fund of knowledge. Our sessions, often with another GAP member, could go far into the night. For me it was the intellectual excitement of a forum in which each could express our most "far out" ideas with the knowledge the other was listening carefully and a thoughtful response would be forthcoming. We talked about what pyschiatry should do, what it could or could not permit, and ways new ideas could be implemented into research. Al was casual and open and easy to know. He would chuckle about the foibles of psychiatry and society rather than get anxious and start sermonizing. In late 1958 when I knew my NIMH research would end in July 1959, it was only an administrative quirk that prevented my moving my family research to Scheflen's institution in Philadelphia. In the years that followed there was a close social relationship between our families. The eight Scheflen children spanned the ages of the four Bowen children. He moved his family to a suburban farm and he became a farmer, more to provide his children with projects to pay their way through college than for his own farm interests. The Scheflen farm with its 200-year-old house was a favorite visiting place for my family. The close family relationship was not possible after his year at the Institute for Advanced Study in Palo Alto and his subsequent move to New York, but my personal and professional relationship with Al continued.

Scheflen had as many personal foibles and "pathologies" as the rest of us but as a thinker, theoretician, and researcher he was one of a few. I agree with him that the final understanding of schizophrenia will not be possible until we have a new paradigm or a new way of thinking. It can require 50 to 200 years for a new paradigm to be woven into the accepted fabric of society. Until the new paradigm is accepted, science tends to focus on phenomenological segments of the problem. Scheflen spoke of the three major paradigms of psychiatry—biology, psychology and sociology. These three separate ways of thinking exist in conceptual isolation from each other. The phenomenon of schizophrenia is defined by a biological, or medical, or *cause* and *effect* model. The medical model has been sufficiently successful that medicine has not had the stimulus for more than superficial change in conceptualizing disease of the body. Psychiatry has had a conceptual enigma with schizophrenia. Some 40 years ago it was conceptualized as having a psychological cause with a psychological theory designed to fit the biological model. The fit was inaccurate and the therapy based on the theory not very effective. By the early 1970s psychiatry, with its "either-or" Aristotelian thinking, had negated psychotherapy as not scientific and it was moving strongly back to the original biological paradigm. During the late 1970s, Scheflen began his effort to integrate all three paradigms with general systems theory.

Some of my experience with schizophrenia will help to understand Scheflen's effort. In the 1950s when I was working on schizophrenia as a family phenomenon I did a paper which contained a statement that the final understanding of schizophrenia would not be possible until we could account for the facts of biology, biochemistry, neurophysiology, psychology, relationships and genetics with a single conceptual frame of reference. There were established *facts* about schizophrenia in each professional discipline. I had no idea how this integration might occur. I was guessing it might require a century or two. I did not understand systems theory at the time. The total family provided a fertile field for systems observations. I set out to develop a family systems theory based on the model of systems in nature. My effort was based on a hunch that this might lead to a new theory of mental illness at some time in the far distant future.

Scheflen followed a different path. He acquired extensive knowledge in each of the three paradigms. Along the way he also acquired extensive knowledge about general systems theory. Then came his effort to begin putting it all together with systems concepts.

I believe *Levels of Schizophrenia* will eventually become one of the important books in the field. I believe systems thinking knows the way through the enigma of schizophrenia. Scheflen did not find definitive answers but he was among the first to point us in a new direction. It is unfortunate he did not have more years to work on this problem before going to publication, but fortunate he had the motivation and energy to complete the book when he knew his life would be limited. His writing is not as clear and concise as it would otherwise have been, but the world will be richer for his final effort.

MURRAY BOWEN, M.D.
Clinical Professor and Director,
Georgetown Family Center;
Department of Psychiatry,
Georgetown University Medical Center,
Washington, D.C.

Contents

10. SUMMARY: THE NATURE AND DEVELOPMENT OF
        SCHIZOPHRENIA 152

    *Epilogue: Some Comments on the Treatment of
        Schizophrenia* 159

    References 163

    Index 167

Preface

Some of you may be interested in how this volume came into being. I will make it brief.

For over 30 years I have chased the elusive issues of schizophrenia. I spent over a decade in neuropathology and neurophysiology. For the next decade I trained in psychoanalysis and psychiatry, working mainly with psychotic people. And then I spent well over a decade studying communication and family organization—always with an eye to the problems of schizophrenic people and their families. So I gained a broad experience at many levels of analysis. But I had no way to put these experiences together.

A few years ago I read a thorough review of current research in schizophrenia (Gunderson et al., 1974). It covered many sciences and ended up with a statement of resignation. There is no way, the authors said, to put all of this together. All the king's horses and all the king's men couldn't put humpty-dumpty together again. Our reductive sciences have led us to a plethora of separate conclusions.

The Gunderson article to me presented a challenge. We are now in a systems age. Why can't we distinguish levels, locate our data and show the interrelationships of levels? I decided to brush up on the neurosciences. I read Carlsson's review of the dopamine hypothesis (1978), Ornstein's presentation on cerebral dominance (1977), and Pribram's remarkable synthesis of neurophysiology and cognitive psychology (1971). Although I gained a vague sense of some connections, there were still too many missing links.

I talked about the problem with a close friend. She gave me a copy of Jaynes' book (1976) on the origins of consciousness, from which I gained a view of how social and cognitive processes were interconnected in schizophrenia. Suddenly I had the idea that I must find and reread a paper by Leaton (1975) on the limbic system. Then the image of the organization of this whole volume came to me. The image had about eight horizontal lines, which represented levels of organization from the societal to the metabolic. I began to fill in old and new ideas about schizophrenia on each line. I had some vague notions about how the levels were interconnected, so I jotted down some notes about these links. It took me about 18 months to find words for this image. In the process I have become convinced that we cannot understand schizophrenia and psychosis without a view of each of these levels of analysis.

The book is sketchy in places and some links are far from certain. I hope that in the future my colleagues will be able to fill out the picture in a more substantial way.

ACKNOWLEDGMENTS

There is no way to acknowledge all of the papers and people who have contributed to my effort. But I do remember that O. Spurgeon English, John Rosen, Catharine Bacon and Warren Hampe helped me to understand the psychodynamic approach to schizophrenia. George Devereaux, Ray Birdwhistell and Gregory Bateson helped me to understand communication and the new epistemology of cybernetics and systems. Murray Bowen, Carl Whitaker and Kitty La Perriere shared their experiences with families which had schizophrenic members. Norman Ashcraft and Andrew and June Ferber aided me in understanding the social aspects of schizophrenia. I have already mentioned some authors who helped me understand the neurophysiology of the problem and I will mention others later.

Susan Barrows, Kitty La Perriere and Norman Ashcraft also helped me with the manuscript. Bernard Mazel supported the conception and its development.

Introduction

In the old days we used to take everything apart in order to do science. We ended up with a bunch of parts or a long list of factors or variables. Then we somehow chose one of them and said *this* is the essence or the main thing or the cause of it all.

This reductionism fragmented science. In the sciences of living systems we ended up with three competing paradigms—social, psychological, and biological. Each of these in turn was split into many subsciences and even within a given science a great many competing theories were developed. Each theory was advocated by a separate school of thought. In the case of schizophrenia, for instance, we had causal theories about the society, the mental hospital, the family, the possessive mother, the weak ego, the adrenals, the nerve potential, the indoles and so on.

Although we were taught to do science this way, it did not entirely escape us that great scientists moved in an integrative direction. Darwin, Maxwell, Weinger, Freud and Einstein painstakingly collected pieces of a puzzle and fitted them together to provide us with a view or pattern. It gradually became apparent that a living entity is not made up of separate elements or independent variables. We slowly began to put the bits together. We started at first with simple correlations and we gradually learned how to view the organization of a field or a system.

By 1920 scientists could talk about homeostasis and about the structure of language. By the 1940s it was possible to imagine retroactive and multiple causation. By the 1950s social scientists could describe the organization of social institutions and the integration of coded events in a communicational process. Endocrine relationships, neural fields and pathways of metabolism were envisioned. As neurophysiologists moved from the study of single neurones to patterns of neural activity, we gained glimpses of cerebral organization and cortical corebrain relationships.

In the 1940s, very different ways of thinking about the human sciences began to emerge, particularly the general system theory of von Bertalanffy (1968) and cybernetics (Weiner, 1948). These new perspectives allowed us to look at complex phenomena like schizophrenia in a new way, considering manifestations of the disorder on different levels, and to abandon linear thinking. By the late 1950s these epistemologically different views had produced a host of new approaches in all the sciences, including neurosciences, social sciences and psychology, and had resulted in a variety of new ideas about schizophrenia.

General systems theory led to integrated views of processes at each of many levels of organization, which allowed us some new postulates about schizophrenia. We could say something about the relationship between schizophrenic behavior and the practices of the mental hospital. A vague picture emerged of communicational deviation in families with a schizophrenic member. We made a few observations about the mother-infant relationship in cases of autism. At about the same time neurophysiologists realized that some difficulty in the metabolism of catecholamines was associated with the psychosis of schizophrenia.

In sum, by the mid-seventies we had achieved a number of new leads about the dysfunction of schizophrenia at about six or seven different levels of organization. It was clear that schizophrenia did not have an essential level of disorder or a single cause. It was necessary to clarify multiple levels of dysfunction and to show how these were interrelated, to identify mutually sustaining loops which could amplify in the development of the child who would become schizophrenic and psychotic.

In the later 1970s new concepts which bridged our views of separate levels were presented. For example, Jaynes (1976) described a theory of the relationship among social dependency, consciousness and hallucinations in ancient peoples. There were further ideas about the importance of the mother-child relationship in the family with a schizophrenic member and some data about the importance of eye contact, voicing and touch in the development of the child. Some data emerged about the relation of learning to the development of dendritic synapses in neural fields. The role of the limbic system in cerebral corebrain relationship was clarified. Meanwhile it was discovered that norepinephrine and dopamine were critical neurotransmitters in temporal and limbic activity.

We do not have all of the pieces of this puzzle and some of the pieces we have are of uncertain validity. But we now have some data at each of many levels and we have conceptual methods for depicting relationships between levels. It is time, then, to make a start. It is time to attempt an integrated picture of schizophrenia at many levels.

In this volume, as I attempt such an integration, I deal at least in passing with a total of about eight levels of processes, from the societal to the molecular. The first part of the book consists of four chapters on society, institutions, family, and mother-infant dyads in relationship to schizophrenia. The second part deals with organismic levels focusing on body states and emotionality and then going on to deal with physiological subsystems. In Part III, I will deal with the revolution in the neurosciences which has enabled us to understand, to some degree, the nueropsychological organization of the nervous system and the organization of the neural microstructure and its metabolism. All of these levels interact in cyclical fashion in schizophrenia.

The new leads I have mentioned in this introduction are, of course, reviewed and referenced in the text. But I also weave into the tapestry many of our old views of cognition and the psychodynamics of schizophrenia, since the new epistemology of integration does not require us to throw away all of the experience we have acquired in the past. Another advantage of this integrating perspective is that, once we have laid out a picture of multiple levels of dysfunction, we can easily draw a picture of how an instance of schizophrenia could develop and be amplified in the life history of the schizophrenic person. Then we can better visualize and plan a multi-level treatment approach. My views on the development and treatment of schizophrenia are given in the final section of this volume.

Levels of Schizophrenia

Part I

Social Levels in Schizophrenia

Until the sixteenth century we employed metaphysical and religious explanations for schizophrenia. Some of these are still used today—by schizophrenic people and their relatives, for instance. In academic circles Western explanations are usually biological, psychological or social. This trichotomy of conceptions leads us to some very simplistic and one-sided notions. Biological and psychological explanations often regard schizophrenia as an intrinsic state of the schizophrenic person, as if he or she grew up in a vacuum apart from relationships and a social order. On the other hand, some zealous social thinkers simply blame schizophrenia on society or its institutions (Goffman, 1961; Szasz, 1963). To gain a more comprehensive view we should gather what information we have about the relations of schizophrenia to social order.

There is no agreed upon way to distinguish social levels of organization. I will deal with the following four levels: 1) the level of society ; 2) the level of our social institutions; 3) the level of primary co-living groups, such as the family; and 4) the level of face-to-face dyadic interaction in the mother-child relationship.

1

The Societal Perspective on Psychosis and Schizophrenia

In the tradition of Western thought we begin a discussion with a definition of the subject matter. We specify the phenomenon in question and locate it in a classificational category. Sometimes we add a statement of explanation or cause.

When we try to do this with psychosis and schizophrenia we are quickly lost in controversy. We do not agree about the cardinal features of the condition or about the boundaries of its occurrence. We do not even agree about whether psychosis and schizophrenia are the same thing or whether either of these is an entity. We cannot decide if these conditions belong to the class of diseases, psychological disturbances, or social disorders. And we have as many explanations as we have specialties and schools of thought.

But we must begin someplace. Is there a relatively neutral statement that allows us a measure of accord?

I think there is. We can probably agree that *psychosis and schizophrenia involve behavior which is deviant from the norms or expectations of our civilization.* This statement does not imply that schizophrenia is only a social deviation; nor does it imply that schizophrenia is the only deviation of our society. Further, it does not offer a cause or an explanation. However, for the moment let us begin by saying that the behavior of psychosis and schizophrenia is deviant and postpone the classificatory and explanatory aspects of our definition.

Even though we have made this restriction, we still face a difficult task in defining this phenomenon. We must ask whether psychosis and insanity and madness and schizophrenia are equivalent terms. If they are not, we must say what differences are connoted by the labels. And we must specify as best we can how this class of deviations is distinguished from other deviations from our societal standards.

This task is sometimes tackled by a discussion of views. I could say, for instance, what these words mean to me, but others would likely have a different perspective. So we will probably not make much progress toward a definition in this way. We must try instead to say how these concepts have already been defined in the traditions of Western civilization. In the lingo of science, we must define our terms on an operational basis. We must try to say what conceptions and standards have interacted with the observable phenomena of psychosis and schizophrenia.

In a crude way, we can do this by comparing the behaviors of psychosis and schizophrenia in the social contexts of historical eras and different contemporary societies. In systems parlance, this effort will take us to a view of the broadest contexts of the issue—to the level of societal organization. My review will hardly scratch the surface of this line of study. To be more exhaustive I would have to deal with many terms and facets of psychosis and I would have to make cross-cultural comparisons beyond a few eras in a few Western societies. But even an abbreviated study will show the relevance of social orders for the understanding of schizophrenia and psychosis and allow us a working definition from which we can proceed to a study of other levels.

It is sometimes assumed that the terms "madness," "psychosis" and "schizophrenia" are synonyms in various eras for the condition we now call "schizophrenia." I think this is not the case, for even though these terms may define somewhat the same deviations they also attest to vast differences in historical eras and cultural perspectives. If we review these differences, we can grasp an important aspect of the relativity of the concept "schizophrenia." It is essential to do this. *In my view, a failure to distinguish between schizophrenia and the psychosis of schizophrenia is a major source of our confusion and disagreement.*

MADNESS AND INSANITY IN THE EARLIER HISTORY OF WESTERN CIVILIZATION

We have no written records of madness before the advent of the ancient Eurasian civilizations, so we do not know what psychotic-like states occurred in the older tribal societies. Although it might be possible to make some inferences about tribal madness from accounts of such societies in relatively underdeveloped countries of the present world, I will confine my account here to the historical period of Western societies.

Instances of madness were reported about 3,000 years ago in Babylon, India, pre-Athenian Greece and ancient Israel. It was written, for instance, that Menelaus of Sparta put his own sheep to the sword in a fit of rage. Nebuchadnezzar was considered mad when he was observed to eat grass and Ezekiel was so judged when he ate his own feces.

Such instances of madness had certain regular features. They were marked by bizarre behavior which was often of the kind we attribute to non-human animals, and they were associated with immoderate affectivity such as rage or grief. Madness seems to have occurred in situations of marked frustration. If the ancient madmen stayed mad for a lifetime we are not told about it. It is notable, too, that madness was not necessarily associated with hallucinations in those days. If hallucinations occurred, they were not considered deviant. Ezekiel saw visions, for instance, but this was not considered a part of his madness.

The social organization of these Eurasian chiefdoms was characterized by an absolute hierarchy of control. Many people were controlled by family and clan patriarchs, who were, in turn, merely serfs to taskmasters, military commanders and officials of the court. The monarchy was absolute in its power over subjects, but the monarch was, in turn, responsible to a powerful priesthood and a hierarchy of gods. These chiefdoms apparently emerged with the population explosion that accompanied agricultural evolution about 5,000 years ago. With this evolutionary event, large numbers of people were freed from immediate food production and hunting, so a large standing army, a large priestly cult and a huge bureaucracy emerged. Many citizens became part of an unfamiliar and complex society. On one hand they were controlled in an absolute chain of command, yet they were separated from the continuous face-to-face contacts with family and clan members typical of tribal society. Possibly this situation engendered both a marked degree of frustration and a lack of immediate family supports for some of the more mobile members of those societies.

Until recently, we have had virtually no hint of the organization of cognitive experience in those civilizations. However, since we now have at least a serious hypothesis on the matter, it is worthwhile to say what we can about this context of madness.

Julian Jaynes (1976) has documented some indications about cognition and social dependency during this era of history. In the ancient, authoritarian chiefdoms, people apparently depended upon the vocal commands and the gaze of authoritarian figures in order to carry out complex, sequential tasks. When a citizen of these societies was separated from an authority figure, he would hallucinate the voice of command and the gaze of social control.

From these observations Jaynes infers that people in a hierarchical chiefdom lacked the ability to do sequential tasks without commands at each step of the procedure. He calls this cognitive state a "bicameral mind." In contemporary language we might speak of it as a cognitive deficiency, a lack of ego strength, a failure to have ego differentiation. From a social standpoint we could regard the people of these ancient civilizations as being dependent on authoritarian chains of command for the maintenance of cognitive organization for complex linear tasks. If this was the case, we are not surprised that hallucinations were not considered deviant. They could occur at any separation. In fact, they would be "normal" at a break in the usual chain of command.

Jaynes goes on to liken ancient people with "bicameral minds" to the people we nowadays term "schizophrenic." I will later argue that schizophrenic people frequently do hallucinate and experience cognitive disorganization when they are separated from parents or "symbiotic" partners or removed from highly structured situations.

About 1000 B.C., the ancient chiefdoms began to break up in parts of Eurasia. According to Jaynes (1976), this political fragmentation was accompanied by a breakdown in the bicameral type of cognition and the emergence of a more modern form of Western consciousness. Urban people, at least, began to be able to sequence complex tasks without endless commands, and hallucinations were no longer generally considered normal or divine (except in rural areas such as Judea and Macedonia).

A few centuries later city-state governments emerged in the Mediterranean region. Governance was relatively more democratic and dialogue replaced authoritarian commands, at least in the patrician levels of society. At the same time, linear activities such as writing and arithmetic calculations evolved. Language, until this time used primarily to list assets or promulgate rules, took the form of discourse and artistic exposition. During this Greco-Roman era more and more citizens learned to read, write, calculate and engage in solitary intellectual pursuits.

It is noteworthy that the Greeks of that era reported many instances of melancholia, which they treated with measures not unlike those of contemporary psychotherapy. Melancholia was not accompanied by overt rage and was not usually characterized by grossly bizarre, unhuman forms of behavior.

During the Middle Ages this ancient cycle of evolution was in some ways repeated. Feudalism returned to Europe and absolute theocracies and monarchies reduced most citizens to serfdom. Again there were reports of madness characterized by rage and very bizarre acts and once again hallucinations were attributed a divine origin. And once again there emerged a Renaissance—a period of relative democracy and less authoritarian societies. Whether or not there was an actual increase in madness during the Renaissance we do not know. Certainly more attention was paid to the matter. There are many accounts of efforts to deal with a considerable number of bizarre, indigent and alienated people. It is possible, however, that this reflected a breakdown of family, clan and feudal responsibility for the insane, rather than a change in the incidence of madness.

Let us look at the social contexts of Western societies during the Renaissance. In the fifteenth century a marked evolution occurred in the social organization of Europe. The upshot of it was the appearance of smaller and smaller family and household units and a great increase in both geographic and social mobility. Trade, travel, conquest and colonialism took millions of Europeans away from family and clan. Meanwhile, the traditional extended household of 15 to 70 people began to break up into separate nuclear family units. Romantic love glorified the dyad. Protestantism placed emphasis on the relationship of the individual and his God instead of loyalty to the church and family hierarchies. More and more socially isolated people appeared in the streets and rooming houses of urban Europe.

Late in the Renaissance hallucinations were again regarded as abnormal. Craziness identified strange, unsuccessful and isolated people who did not necessarily show rage or any other emotion. Their strangeness was characterized by foolishness, wandering and weird self-accounts. People who behaved like non-human animals still appeared, but the boundaries of madness were now more inclusive.

In sum, the form and definition of madness seem to have differed with the form of societal organization. More precisely, it seems to have varied with the intactness of family and clan relationships and the absoluteness of pyramidal organizations.

INDUSTRIAL SOCIETIES AND THE EMERGENCE OF THE CONCEPT OF SCHIZOPHRENIA

Western civilization experienced the industrial revolution in two waves. The first occurred with the Renaissance as early as the fifteenth century. The second began in the nineteenth century and continues still. This line of social evolution seems to be related to the form and occurrence of psychosis and schizophrenia.

Industrialization and colonialism demand a large number of people who can be highly mobile without depression or the loss of cognitive skills. In industrialized societies wealth and fame come to those who are willing to leave their families and travel to the more remote regions of the globe. *It becomes a virtue to accomplish social mobility without psychosis.* Presumably, those who cannot do so stay quietly at home or are taken into membership in a total institution like the monastery, the military, or the asylum.

After the Renaissance, Western philosophers rationalized and glorified social mobility. Individualism became a Western value. Later, the theorists of mental health continued this glorification, proposing that those who were most individualistic and mobile were mature and mentally healthy. Those who experienced immoderate emotionality or cognitive disorganization in social isolation were regarded as immature, deviant or mentally ill. By the 1930s even those with close ties to a parent or a spouse were said to be "overdependent" or "orally regressive."

In the nineteenth century, madness became increasingly the subject of medical jurisdiction and neurological research. In addition, the relevance of disorders of consciousness became of increasing interest in jurisprudence. In these institutional contexts bizarreness was given a variety of names, reflecting various theories about its nature and significance. The term "madness" was employed less and less—possibly because rage was a less evident feature of the deviance. The term "insanity" was often employed on the basis that it was a less stigmatic euphemism. The term "lunacy" was widely used on the basis that insanity was a result of being moon-stricken. At the same time, the medical emphasis on psychosis as a disease of the brain led to the coining of terms such as "paraphrenia." Since it was the usual practice to incarcerate bizarre people, the picture of chronic institutionalization became more and more intertwined with the picture of madness.

In the twentieth century, the industrialization of Western nations continued, along with the breakdown of family cohesiveness. Mothers began to be away from home during working hours. The educational system began to take more and more responsibility for the cognitive abilities of the child. It eventually would take responsibility for his emotional maturation and social adjustment as well.

I do not think it was any accident that the concept of schizophrenia evolved at the turn of the twentieth century. Suppose we examine this development and relate it to the social contexts I have been sketching.

Just after 1900, a Swiss psychiatrist named Bleuler (1950) coined the term schizophrenia, which has since become accepted throughout the Western world. Bleuler based the diagnosis of schizophrenia upon three characteristics which can be mnemonically coded the three "A"s: looseness of *associations*; a flattening of *affect*; and social or emotional *ambivalence*. We might nowadays state these criteria in slightly different terms, saying that a looseness of associations is a relative difficulty in sequencing linear activities such as exposition, narration, calculations and motor actions, that a flatness of affect is an inadequacy of emotional response, and that ambivalence is a conflicting tendency for overdependency on the one hand and alienation on the other.

Bleuler did not include hallucinations and delusions in his list of necessary criteria. He regarded these as secondary manifestations of schizophrenia.

The Bleulerian approach gained broad acceptance in America, particularly among those clinicians with a psychological orientation. In fact, after about 1930 a Bleulerian view of criteria for schizophrenia and a psychodynamic view of mental disorders became widely influential in American psychology and education.

Meanwhile, the emphasis on geographic mobility and the decreasing size and influence of the family continued. Now over half of American women are employed outside the household. The school takes increasing responsibility for evaluating our children and fostering their development. And in spite of complaints about the lowered standards of education, our children are still expected to accomplish independent linear tasks by late childhood. In fact, a relative inability at such skills is dealt with by lamentation, by special programs of education and by ascriptions of deficit and abnormality.

At this writing, a child with markedly substandard performance in linear skills, together with low emotionality and low sociability, is likely to be labeled "borderline schizophrenic" or perceived as being at "high risk" for a later psychosis.

In summary, our contemporary category of schizophrenia is much more inclusive than old categories such as madness and insanity. This broadening seems to reflect the demanding standards of an industrial society for greater mobility and for greater abilities in cognitive sequencing and emotional modulation.

CULTURAL DIFFERENCES IN THE DIAGNOSIS OF SCHIZOPHRENIA

In recent centuries the definitions of psychosis and schizophrenia have been largely entrusted to psychiatric and related disciplines. The general population in some measure takes its views from these professions. It is interesting to note that diagnostic categories differ noticeably from one nation or one culture to another. I will discuss here only two major traditions of diagnosis and conception.

The Bleulerian tradition of diagnosis did take hold in psychodynamic circles in America and in some other nations, such as Britain. But acceptance was far from universal. Another very different conception, which also developed at the turn of the century, has become predominant in Northern Europe, in the more biological disciplines of America and even in Bleuler's Switzerland. This tradition of diagnosis and definition is so different from contemporary versions of Bleuler theory that it is difficult to imagine that the two views are describing the same condition.

Differences in Views of Cognitive Disorder

In the Kraepelinian (1906) tradition, the diagnosis of schizophrenia rests upon the finding of severe cognitive disorders such as delusions and hallucinations. Schneider (1959), for example, calls these "first-rank symptoms." The diagnosis of schizophrenia is not made unless these dysfunctions appear. Also, in this tradition the diagnosis is based upon an unrelenting course of progressive psychotic deterioration, so nonpsychotic states are not countenanced in the diagnosis of schizophrenia.

Some contemporary German clinicians (e.g., Jaspers, 1963) also believe that the schizophrenic patient cannot be reached for rapport or social contact. In their view this unreachability is one of the diagnostic criteria. To the Kraepelinians, then, the schizophrenic is a deluded, hallucinating, unreachable person who will probably become more and more psychotic without remission.

The Bleulerian conception of schizophrenia is in some ways dia-metrically opposed to the Kraepelinian. Less serious difficulties in organizing thoughts and associations are noted as cardinal symptoms of schizophrenia in the Bleulerian tradition, *but delusions and hallu-cinations are regarded as secondary manifestations*. The contempor-ary psychodynamic clinicians who have leaned to Bleuler's view also pay much more attention to emotionality and social relatedness. They do not regard the prognosis to be that of a progressive disease. Instead, they see the possibility of remissions and non-psychotic states of schizophrenia. Also, in this tradition the schizophrenic is in no way regarded as unreachable.

In short, one tradition regards psychosis as a necessary criterion for the definition of schizophrenia, while in the other schizophrenia is regarded as a state in which psychosis may occur as a complication or episodic state. As we will see, these differences in conception inspire and sustain a quite different approach to the schizophrenic person. And these differences in approach in turn support the diag-nostic criteria.

It seems probable that these differences in definition relate to cultural differences in German and American society. Certainly the Germans have clung more closely to a biological and medical con-ception of schizophrenia, while many American clinicians have taken a psychoanalytic orientation. It is also the case that Germany has a more autocratic tradition of governance than Switzerland or the United States. Possibly more attention is paid to hallucinations in a state which is more recently emerging from strict autocracy. Possibly, too, a society with stronger family ties and an authoritarian structure pays less attention to peer relationships and adjustments outside of the family. If so, less attention might be paid as well to the social relationships of the schizophrenic patient. I cannot do any more than make conjectures in these matters. Someday they may be studied in detail.

The Problem of Emotional Modulation

Emotionality is an aspect of schizophrenic behavior which is more clearly based upon ethnic and regional differences. Bleuler considered the absence of evident emotionality to be a cardinal symptom of schizophrenia but in the Kraepelinian tradition less attention is paid to emotionality. In fact, if the psychotic patient is emotionally labile he is classed as a manic-depressive rather than a schizophrenic.

American clinicians, who tend to pay a great deal of attention to emotion in general, make it an important aspect of the diagnosis of schizophrenia. But here there is a problem in the Bleulerian criteria. Many patients who are otherwise classified as schizophrenics do not show a flat affectivity. On the contrary, as in ancient madness, there is excessive rage or depression or elation. They undermodulate affectivity rather than overcontrolling it. Because of this the old categories have been amended to introduce a category called "schizoaffective schizophrenia."

Most clinicians pay little attention to the ethnic background of a schizophrenic person. Accordingly, it was belatedly noticed that many emotionally labile people with schizophrenic problems of cognition came from Central Europe or the Mediterranean. It is, of course, nowadays evident that emotional suppression is not a valued or normal trait except in Northern European cultures. Hispanic people, for example, show rage and grief quite demonstrably in a crisis. Many American clinicians who do not realize this use the diagnosis of schizophrenia or hysteria quite indiscriminately when they see Hispanic patients.

It seems obvious that we can get above the problem of arguing about whether schizophrenia is a flatness or an excess of affectivity. We must take a cultural perspective beyond that of Northern European, British and American norms. We observe that marked disorders of emotionality can occur in either direction. Then we can say that a marked disorder *in the modulation* of affect occurs in schizophrenia resulting in an imbalance that exceeds the norms of any society.

In sum, we have very different conceptions of schizophrenia and psychosis in various traditions of diagnosis. These differences have evolved in divergent directions in different Western societies, but they are also related to scientific discipline and social class. It is worth noting that our diagnostic criteria are primarily Northern European in origin and middle-class in their professional applications. It is not surprising that they feature a close attention to cognitive organization and emotional modulation. It is also not surprising that American versions feature an attention to social relatedness.

A CULTURE OF PSYCHOTIC LORE

To say that the norms and values of a society define its deviations is to present only one side of the coin. So I must introduce an additional perspective here that I will try to clarify in successive chapters. *The occurrence of madness and the conceptions we have of it also influence the general social order.* In fact, the definitions of deviance and social order are mutually sustaining. Let me begin to spell out what I mean by this and take up the theme again in Chapters 2 and 3.

It is a terrifying experience to become psychotic. It is also terrifying to be approached by bizarre or assaultive psychotic people. So a fear of psychosis is widespread in our societies. This fear is enhanced by the lack of adequate explanations for psychosis and by the widely accepted view that the prognosis for the psychotic is hopeless.

Many of the different formulations of madness which have been made over the centuries have a common theme. Madness is associated with an excess of passion, while other forms of psychosis are associated with its absence—with zombie-like states. In either state there is an implication of the loss of control. In the extreme form, myth has it that any of us could go mad and commit heinous crimes without realizing it. Or any of us could fall under the spell of a wicked wizard and become helpless thralls of his bidding.

Schizophrenic people are not more violent than the general population and sexuality is rarely a preoccupation of psychotic people. But this is not how the man in the streets views psychosis. On the contrary, it is often believed that the mental hospital is a place of unrelenting and uncontrolled violence and sex. A few years ago I hailed a taxi and asked the driver to take me to a well-known private hospital in Philadelphia. The driver reluctantly agreed, but insisted upon leaving me a block from the main entrance. He said he would not go closer to this insane asylum. I told him that the people there were not violent but more peaceful and less homicidal than those who lived in the adjacent neighborhoods. His response surprised me. He said, "It's not the violence. It's the sex." He went on to tell me that in his view the inmates were continuously having strange and bizarre kinds of sex.

The idea of a loss of control is associated with another belief about schizophrenia. The schizophrenic person is commonly regarded as lacking in character, will or morality. He is weak so we castigate him or we overprotect him. This notion of weakness is fortified by old and recent doctrines of psychiatry. In the old French school the psychotic was seen as a moral degenerate, a view which was widespread in the nineteenth century. Now biologists speak of a metabolic deficiency, while psychologists speak of cognitive deficiency, ego weakness and so on. Some contemporary family therapists hold that schizophrenia is an "emotional weakness" passed down in successive generations of some families (Bowen, 1978b).

So there is a moral aspect to the problem of schizophrenia. One should stand on one's own two feet. Or, in a more authoritarian tradition, one should listen to one's parents and all other duly constituted authority. Each schizophrenic heard one of these instructions almost interminably as he or she was growing up. Schizophrenics may say it themselves, too, revealing an immense sense of inferiority or sometimes a reactive grandiosity.

So what is the moral? I think it is this: "Obey. Mind your p's and q's. Develop your character or else." "Or else what?" "Or else you too may become psychotic like your Uncle Joe or your Aunt Mary."

Erikson (1966) has postulated that deviance is critical for maintaining social cohesion and for exemplifying the desirable stereotypes of our traditions. How does one teach a boy to be clean without dirty boys to point to? How do we define social norms without public instances of deviation?

All of our experiences with the bizarreness of psychosis and all of our mystifying explanations of it form a lore. Intertwined in this lore are our collective fears of sexuality, violence, perversion, enslavement and loss of control—all of this embellished by a myriad of stories about the strange and the weird. Added to these myths is what we do know about schizophrenia. This lore is universal in our culture and passed down from generation to generation as part of our cultural heritage.

Among other things, this lore is used to frighten children and adults. It is part of the indoctrination to the moralities of obedience and self-control. So our conceptions of schizophrenia not only arise from the nature of our social order, but *also serve to maintain it.* The frightening begins in the family, but is contained in our school system, along with the distinction between normal and deviant children. The slower learner, the less social child, or the child prone to excessive emotionality is singled out in school and neighborhood. Odious comparisons are made. Punishments, criticism and ostracism may be meted out. However, such a child is also given a measure of preferential treatment. Special classes are convened, rigid rules are relaxed and exceptions are made. The humanistic teacher even intercedes for the deviant pupil with higher authorities and unsympathetic parents.

Once a child is labeled as deviant, a set of secondary reinforcements can fix and direct the role. There is now a rationale for poor performance. The child and those around him may stop expecting anything better. And the very deviance which disturbs adults may provide the unusual child with a measure of status among other deviant children. From now on the deviance achieves a direction and a content. The deviant child begins to learn from other children with whom he is classed by the label. Elders unwittingly instruct the child in further deviance, by comparing the child with older deviants in the family, the school, the neighborhood, or those of literary importance.

Such suggestions may have the force of a self-fulfilling prophesy. If little Mary or Johnnie is compared to a psychotic relative who died in the state hospital, the child may grow up with the expectation of a similar fate. If a detached child is compared to Joan of Arc, the child may make an imago of this historical lady and emulate some of her ways. In short, predictions and comparisons can become instructions which inform and shape preoccupations and influence relational modes. They do not on this account cause schizophrenia but they may shape its form and aggravate its deviations.

The prevailing conception of schizophrenia also influences and shapes the behavior of the professionals in a society. Clinicians in the Kraepelinian tradition, who do not believe that a schizophrenic patient is reachable, make little effort to establish rapport. In America, in circles which do not share this belief, a great effort is made to achieve a close relationship with schizophrenic patients. In fact, many American clinicians are taught how to do this. To these clinicians almost all schizophrenic people are reachable. These clinicians even believe that a marked dependency is too readily attained by a schizophrenic client.

Similarly, clinicians who imagine a hopeless prognosis so inform the parents and ultimately the patient learns of this. Accordingly, a self-fulfilling prophecy can emerge. *The practices and the outcomes maintain and verify the preexisting conceptions.*

THE SOCIAL DEFINITION OF PSYCHOSIS AND SCHIZOPHRENIA

We should now review the issues to see if our survey of views and contexts has clarified the definition of psychosis and schizophrenia, but first we must make a distinction that has so far been only implicit.

At the social level, terms like "psychosis" are conceptions, abstractions about a class of people and behaviors. At this level, psychosis or schizophrenia is not a disorder in or of a particular patient. Because of this we must be cautious on two counts: First, to define schizophrenia as a social deviance *is not to deny or discount* the occurrence of a psychological aberration, a problem of neural organization or a metabolic dysfunction of the brain in people with schizophrenia. At this level we are dealing with a perspective of a category. Second, the use of such categories is relative to a tradition of thought and observation. It may be that the schizophrenic person shows certain behaviors that would be dysfunctional or deviant in any era or any culture, *but ways of looking at the categories are relative* to culture, professional discipline and other dimensions of experience.

Bearing these caveats in mind, we can ask about madness, insanity and psychosis. It seems possible to crudely distinguish two sorts of craziness in earlier Western history. In madness, grossly bizarre, animal-like behavior and extreme emotionality are described. This picture is usually reported in highly hierarchical societies. Another syndrome of odd behavior, low affectivity and social isolation is more often reported in more democratic states with weaker clan and family organizations. It is probable that delusions and hallucinations occur in each of these syndromes, though these behaviors were not considered pathological at some eras of history.

The contemporary category of psychosis includes this historical spectrum of deviation, encompassing behavior, thinking, affectivity and social relatedness, but there are several other dimensions of the category. First, the psychosis of schizophrenia is differentiated from other psychotic states that are obviously related to general physiological disorders such as fever, toxicity or detectable brain damage. Secondly, the term "psychosis" suggests gross disturbance of cognition, such as delusions or hallucinations, even when motor behavior is not grossly bizarre. Thirdly, the present conception of psychosis embraces an immodulation of affect and a deviance of social attachments.

In the United States a distinction between psychosis and schizophrenia has slowly evolved. A contemporary view might be that schizophrenia is a nonpsychotic state which is characterized by: 1) less obvious difficulties than those seen in psychosis in carrying out linear and sequential activities of thought, speech and other motor behaviors; 2) a relative difficulty in modulating moods, tonus and attention; and 3) a combination of overdependency on a partner or a field of cues and an alienation from most other people. I will elaborate these definitions in detail in the chapters to come.

Another dimension of the relativity of these categories must be noted. There are degrees of schizophrenia deviance countenanced by terms such as "remission," "borderline" or "at high risk." There are also relative degrees of psychosis. I will later distinguish four stages of psychotic disorganization on the basis of dominant levels of neural organization.

2

Schizophrenia at Institutional Levels

It is blindingly simplistic to suppose that a society is made up of individuals. A society is made up of large institutions which are in turn composed of local and specialized subinstitutions. Even these subinstitutions have levels of organization, for there are face-to-face or primary groups within the institutional organization. For instance, a patient may fall under the aegis of the state mental health system within a particular clinic in which he and his family have an ongoing relationship with a particular therapist.

There is another aspect to the concept of institutions. An institution is also a system of procedures and ideas. In fact, a body of people, actions and beliefs is an institution. So private practice is an institution, even though it may be less closed and less total than the mental hospital. In short, the institution consists of customers and staff and of practices and ideologies. We cannot afford to use the term less broadly if we are to understand the sociology of schizophrenia.

In order to sketch a view of the institutional level of schizophrenia, I shall say that: 1) The control of psychosis is now the province of a huge system of mental health organizations and governmental agencies, but 2) other institutions of our society sustain and use the concept of schizophrenia for a variety of purposes, and (3) these practices collectively control psychosis but sustain schizophrenia.

THE CONTROL OF PSYCHOSIS

About a million Americans are continuing wards of the mental health system. Uncounted others live in some total institution which is not under the jurisdiction of mental health, e.g. the military, the prison system and certain families. Still other psychotic people live in isolation in the interstices of our cities and rural areas.

The Development of Mental Hospitals

Let us focus first on the closed mental institution. As clinicians most of us are familiar with its more overt facets, so I have no intention of describing hospitals in any detail. But there are some less apparent aspects which we often overlook. One way to call attention to these is to look at how this institution came into being. The story is quite revealing.

In the sixteenth century the jurisdiction of madness passed from the church and the family to the medical institutions and governments of Europe. Maybe this passage of jurisdiction would have occurred anyway by a process of evolution, but in fact it was accomplished in a single coup of great political and economic significance. The story has been told in detail by the French historian Foucault (1965). In the mid-sixteenth century a single solution was proposed for several very trying circumstances. More and more isolated people were appearing in the streets of urban Europe. There was a great depression and poverty-stricken rural folks began to move in large numbers to urban centers in hope of finding work or sustenance. In Paris, for example, the streets were crowded with mendicants and more arrived every day from the provinces. The situation was so critical that the King stationed archers at the gates of the city with orders to kill anyone who arrived there without work or money. What could be done about all these hungry and unemployed citizens?

There was a place to put them. In the fourteenth century leprosy had been rampant in Europe. There were about a half-million registered beds for lepers in the leprosoria of Europe; perhaps an equal number were not registered. But in the fifteenth and sixteenth centuries leprosy virtually disappeared, so the leprosoria stood vacant and unused. The French crown came up with a brilliant idea. Why not put psychotic, isolated and poverty-stricken French citizens in the leprosoria? The idea was carried out. Thousands of mendicants were rounded up and institutionalized in Paris within a few weeks. The practice spread across Europe. In only a few years a half-million indigents, madmen, and socially unskilled people were incarcerated in these institutions.

The leprosoria were medical institutions. Diagnoses were used to classify the new inmates. Measures to deal with them were designated as treatments. In subsequent years times improved in Europe and those who had occupational and social skills left the institutions for the job market. Those who were psychotic or less employable were retained.

In the centuries which followed, the practice of institutionalizing indigents and psychotic people continued. Most were thrown unattended into cells and dungeons. About 1800, extensive reforms in the care of these inmates occurred in England and France. The basis of more contemporary procedures was established. From this date on, more and more institutions specifically designated as asylums were built in all Western nations. The resident population of these institutions steadily and relentlessly increased until a generation ago.

Some social institutions are "total." A lifelong membership and sometimes a lifelong residency within the walls of its buildings are expected. In the total institution, a governing cadre exercises almost complete control of the ideation and life activities of its members. To hold membership in a total institution may mean that one holds no other social role. In becoming a priest, for instance, one abrogates the social roles of husband and father.

In the centuries after 1600 the asylum was a total institution. Walled compounds held most inmates for their lifetimes. Almost complete acceptance of the rules and the ideation of the institution was expected of the patients and often of staff members as well. As family members lost interest and inmates became disenfranchised, the role of patient often became the inmates' only role. Since the prognosis was considered hopeless, those inmates who were discharged often retained their institutional roles years after discharge. Reincarceration could occur without due process. The role of psychotic patient was sanctioned and enforced by law.

The care of socially incompetent and psychotic people thus became the province of medicine. At first, physicians regarded madness as an unexplained malady which could be comprehended only by supernatural ideas. In the nineteenth century, however, supernatural explanations were repudiated and a protracted search for the pathology of psychosis was carried out. As this effort failed, a dichotomy arose between "organic illness," which had demonstrated lesions, and "functional illness," which had no discoverable physical disorder. The functional psychoses became the province of psychiatry. It was generally believed that schizophrenia was an organic disease of genetic origin and it was expected that its material cause would someday be found. In the twentieth century a psychological view also developed, which was applied in some circles to the explanation and treatment of schizophrenia. Thus, the dichotomous schools we discussed in Chapter 1 came about.

Since the 1940s many mental health professionals other than psychiatrists have joined in the treatment of psychosis and all of the life sciences have joined the effort to understand it. Changes in procedure have accompanied this inclusion. Now more of the care of schizophrenic patients is carried out in outpatient facilities and clinics. Antipsychotic drugs are extensively used in both inpatient and outpatient facilities.

A contemporary mental hospital with its associated clinics is one subsystem in the large, complex system of mental health agencies and related organizations. Local, state and federal facilities coexist. These are often associated with university departments of psychiatry, psychology and social work with large training research programs. These governmental and academic subsystems are backed up by programs for rehabilitation, drug abuse, alcoholism, and speech training, as well as by a variety of social agencies. These subsystems may also maintain foster homes, sheltered workshops, day hospitals and homes for psychotic and other incapacitated people. In addition, the physicians of a community still have rights to commit mental patients and a number of practicing psychiatrists and psychotherapists more or less cooperate with the public agencies. Lay groups advocate the rights of patients or support the centers of treatment. In short, the mental health movement is now a huge network of associated institutions.

Practices to Reduce Psychosis

The practices of contemporary mental health are more humane and effective than those of past generations. Since the 1950s the number of patients in public mental hospitals has consistently declined for the first time in the history of total institutions. Sometimes credit for this is given solely to the use of antipsychotic drugs, but total programs and greater community tolerance are also important factors. Medications allay panic and may help in the modulation of affectivity. They also aid in the restoration of cognitive organization. Along with drug therapy, hospital practice offers physical constraint and discipline. At the same time, personal contact and the restoration of prepsychotic social ties are fostered. In short, the minimal triad of hospitalization is medication, social control and interpersonal contact.

Intervention in the acute psychosis is often critical in the life history of the schizophrenic patient. Social constraint and the restoration of social connectedness will ordinarily result in a decrease in cognitive disorganization and over-emotionality within a few days or a week. In my view this can often be accomplished without antipsychotic drugs, but these drugs abet and hasten the process. However, when a patient is acutely psychotic, an *inadequate* program may result in a chronic apathetic state of continuing psychosis. Like many American clinicians, I hold that the prognosis is largely a function of what measures are taken. If nothing critical is done, the prognosis of lifelong disability becomes a self-fulfilling prophesy.

There is one other point. The reestablishment of a directive relationship may terminate the psychotic phase of schizophrenia with or without antipsychotic drugs. This does not mean that the more long-lasting schizophrenia is necessarily altered.

When the acute or severe psychosis abates, the patient is discharged from the hospital, frequently to an outpatient facility. Medications may be continued, therapy or rehabilitation programs may be employed, and social skills training is occasionally available. But there are many alternative pathways for psychotic patients. Some do not improve and cannot leave the hospital at all or do so only to be readmitted a few weeks later. Still others leave the hospital system altogether. Of these some are maintained in other total institutions such as prison or a restrictive household, but some return to a useful and active life without manifest deficiencies of the schizophrenic type.

The pathways and eventualities of schizophrenia are numerous and complicated. There are so many interlocking variables that assessment and prediction are almost impossible. Outcomes depend upon patient talent and determination, in relation to family and occupational supports, in relation to available facilities and kinds of therapies and so on. Yet there is a common problem which therapists and patients alike must face, so I will take a moment to describe it.

The Paradox of Treatment and Institutional Dependency

In spite of radical reforms in the procedures of mental hospitals, some continue a practice which characterized all asylums in the nineteenth century. Goffman (1961) describes it as a "rite de passage." The new admission is stripped of clothing and personal possessions and placed in seclusion. Only when he or she becomes docile and cooperative are certain rights and privileges restored. This time-honored practice, decried by humanists and psychotherapists, is not employed in the more liberal hospitals. But there are certain rites of passage in virtually all hospitals. A measure of compliance with ward rules is required. The patient must achieve "insight" or an acceptance that he or she is mentally ill. Discharge may depend upon cooperation with a psychotherapist. Often the patient must accept a role in follow-up or aftercare programs. Finally, an official diagnosis is made and recorded.

These procedures can be regarded as an induction into the role of mental patient within the institution of mental health. They can also be interpreted as necessary compliance to a position of dependent reliance on the personnel, the practices and the ideologies of this institutional system.

I am not suggesting that these procedures should be abandoned. In fact, it seems that the termination of a severe psychotic state may depend in large measure upon the acceptance of a dependent relationship. I am saying only that this dependency maintains a state of affairs that has existed for the schizophrenic person long before hospitalization. So we face a paradox. The measures used to terminate psychosis tend to maintain a dependency upon family, staff members, and institutionalization and to confirm mental health conceptions.

This difficulty persists after discharge from the hospital. In fact, the dependency is maintained for many patients at institutional levels from the household to the clinic (or office) to the agencies of government.

The patient's family—disturbed by the psychosis—may regroup around the patient and make the household into a total institution. Helen, for instance, had been hospitalized several times in a private hospital. The family no longer had funds to pay her bills and was unwilling to cooperate further with her therapists. So the family took Helen home. Someone was always with her. Her parents, who previously had always argued with each other, came to present a united front toward Helen. If she disagreed with them, her disagreement was attributed to her psychosis. If she behaved rebelliously, the father administered extra Thorazine from a large cache of reserves accumulated from other hospitalizations. An eighteenth-century hospital had been established in the home.

In Joe's case the psychiatrist agreed that Joe should be kept at home. He made himself available for emergency calls and prescribed more phenothiazines when the family was anxious about Joe's restlessness. The psychiatrist even trained Joe's mother in some of the procedures of psychiatric nursing. And every year, when the family went on vacation, the psychiatrist had Joe readmitted for two weeks of "observation."

Sometimes the incarceration at home is more malevolent. When Betty was hospitalized, her husband began to go with his secretary. He was persuaded to take his wife home, but he had her watched by the children and he was virtually never home. If she complained he would threaten her with readmission. Betty cooperated with all of this, having marked dependency and an endless self-accusatory viewpoint.

Analogous situations occur in the clinic. Maybe the patient is retained in a day hospital but there is little real activity. Once a day an attendant brings medication. The "psychotherapy," if any, consists of warnings, reassurances and other sorts of maternal or paternal supportiveness. A therapist may attempt insight therapy but there are serious questions about the ability of most therapists to do this with schizophrenic patients. Consequently, most of the available therapists select non-schizophrenic patients for their major efforts.

The problem may be aided and abetted by the way state and other agencies are employed by patients, families and therapists. To receive some kinds of public services, patients may have to be committed or carried on hospital rosters. The maintenance of a patient status may also be necessary to receive welfare or disability pensions. If the patient has no other means of support, few therapists will refuse to sign the necessary papers for welfare and few patients will easily give up government supports. Furthermore, many institutions receive government funds in an amount equivalent to the number of patients carried on the books, so patients are not discharged until the beds or their slots in the outpatient program are filled by other recruits.

Needless to say, such activity conflicts with efforts to regain employment and self-sufficiency. The mental health worker is caught between helping the patient become self-sufficient and "mature" and a wish not to see the client in dire fiscal need (or the hospital, for that matter). So the very systems which are to terminate patienthood become invested in its continuance.

The mental patient is not only dependent on the family or upon one institution. He is caught, so to speak, beneath a canopy of interdependent institutions. In spite of much talk about confidentiality, the records are always obtainable. The diagnosis of schizophrenia accompanies the patient and colors his management in each facility of the network. If a patient with such a diagnosis goes to a medical facility, his credibility is suspect when he complains about symptoms. When he seeks to leave the umbrella, the diagnosis will adversely affect his ability to obtain a job. Even the treatment procedures can be aversive. Large doses of phenothiazines greatly limit mental abilities and can cause crippling side effects.

Even insight psychotherapy can put the schizophrenic person and the therapist in a bind. Here is how this characteristically occurs. Therapy focuses on the patient's obvious problem of dependency and social withdrawal, i.e., upon "the defenses" against social contact and maturation. The very success of these efforts can get the schizophrenic person into serious difficulties. Efforts which succeed in weakening the patient's dependency can result in further cognitive disorganization. Efforts to reduce seclusiveness can lead the patient to seek new attachments which end traumatically in another withdrawal. Consequently, the very therapeutic efforts which are very helpful to a neurotic patient can make matters worse in schizophrenia, particularly if they are not accompanied by ways to improve the social and cognitive abilities of the patient.

A Catch-22

The schizophrenic patient and the humanistic mental health worker are in a Catch-22. The procedures of therapy can backfire and have paradoxical effects. The patient is discharged from the hospital but moves from one total institution to another. If a progressive program succeeds in lowering the hospital census, its funds will be reduced since fiscal support is based upon the number of patients.

Each psychotic episode increases family distance, damages employability or career prospects and enchances pessimism and dependency on others. It is a vicious cycle for many patients. A main cause of psychosis is past psychosis, and each episode can deepen the schizophrenic problem.

Some theorists, such as Goffman (1961) and Szasz (1963), have gone so far as to blame the institutions for schizophrenia. This is not my position. Although the hospital procedures may sustain dependency, the psychotic-to-be has serious difficulty before he or she encounters the mental hospital. Hospitalism ameliorates psychosis, but it usually does not alter the problem of cognition. The mental health system may sustain schizophrenia; however, until now this has been the price of the control of psychosis. Later I will present alternate definitions and procedures. Meanwhile we should take a look at some of the loops of schizophrenia that are larger and longer than the practices of the mental health system.

THE CONCERN OF OTHER INSTITUTIONS WITH PSYCHOSIS AND SCHIZOPHRENIA

Government agencies, legislatures and courts all have an interest in psychotic people and in the conception of schizophrenia. Consider the role of the courts, for instance. Our courts can commit a person to a mental hospital and deprive a diagnosed psychotic of certain civil rights. Many rulings which protect patients and demand equal opportunities for them have also come from the courts.

Most strange, however, is the notion that a psychotic person is to be judged differently in the case of a crime. This practice keeps our courts occupied with the problem of defining psychosis. Further, the opportunity to escape punishment by an insanity plea adds to the lore of schizophrenia and possibly to its maintenance.

The M'Naghten rule holds that a person can be found not guilty of a crime by reason of insanity. The Durham rule even allows a verdict of not guilty if a jury can be convinced that the defendant was possessed by an "irresistible impulse" at the time of the crime. In France a "crime of passion" is very likely to be excused. In short, our legal system considers the loss of conscious control and a marked degree of overriding emotionality as a reason for exoneration, although this proposition has been and will continue to be tested again and again in our courts.

Certainly we can consider this procedure an example of the dedication of our judicial system to the premise that all factors must be aired in order to render a just verdict. But there is more to the issue. It is not simply that psychosis is an extenuating circumstance. One is actually declared not guilty if he is judged insane. It is as though the crime had not been committed. This strange idea seems to stem from the fact that intent is considered necessary for guilt. If one is psychotic there is, presumably, no intent.

Informally, our sanity, our morality and our motives are endlessly being examined and judged by our colleagues in any institution. In a sense, we are on trial in our families, in our cafeterias, in our work places, and in our neighborhoods. The computers of industry and government keep records of every citizen's personal and public life. We now have "trials" of our people by the news media as well. But it is not simply that people are forever being judged. Issues of intent, morality and responsibility are at stake in our judgments of each other's sanity and stability.

The arts, too, review these matters. Novels depict the life struggles of their characters. The play is often the modern equivalent of the medieval "Everyman." Matters of deviance come up in many class-rooms. The media air the problems of mental illness and politicians take issue with the early release of mental patients. Religions are always concerned with morality and the control of passions and many contemporary clergymen are also psychotherapists. In view of the fact that many laymen equate any emotional disturbance or deviancy with psychosis, the problem of psychosis colors all these discussions and reviews.

In my view this interest goes far beyond a humanitarian concern for the schizophrenic person. Issues of psychosis contain concerns about emotional control, social connectedness and the conventional standards of reason. Since these permeate our lives, psychosis plays a major role in the maintenance of our social order. This proposition has already been mentioned in Chapter 1 where I suggested that a fear of psychosis and its use as an example maintain social order and define unacceptable deviance.

There is little agreement within or among different societal insti-tutions about the nature of schizophrenia. No consensus has been reached in the legal system, the arts, the schools, and/or religions. Why is this so?

Ambiguities

Possibly there is more to the matter. Why do we not have a single theory of schizophrenia or a unified procedure for dealing with social transgressions? Why do our religions balance a punitive and a for-giving approach? From a standpoint of the equilibrium of a system, we can give a general answer.

It is often said in a democracy that war is too important and dangerous to be left to the generals. Maybe we should say this about schizophrenia too. Maybe it is important not to resolve such issues by the dominance of one school of thought. If consensus is reached around a simplistic proposition, it may not stand the test of time, and in the past our institutions have carried out some horrendous excesses on the basis of a temporary consensus and the power it allows. The burning of hundreds of thousands of "witches" is an example. So are the crusades. And so was the genocide of the Third Reich.

Even in an autocracy, a measure of national sanity and the avoidance of excesses depend upon a balance of institutions like religion and government. In a democracy we consider a system of checks and balances to be critical in the preservation of the system. This concept of equilibrium goes for ideologies as well as for branches of government. In systems terms, the equilibrium of a system is maintained by a number of mutually corrective or balancing processes.

The Utility of a Psychiatric Diagnosis

These views of the role of schizophrenia in the preservation of social order are quite debatable, but it is difficult to doubt the social usefulness of a psychiatric or legal diagnosis. There are at least three such uses.

1) *The Right to Incarcerate Non-Criminal, But Difficult People.* In our society we do not allow the incarceration of citizens who have not committed a crime. Those who might do so and those who are otherwise difficult to contend with are therefore not controllable by due process. The institutionalization of deviants provides a means for the social control of those who have not committed a crime.

As I noted above, endless trials about culpability and insanity maintain a distinction between psychosis and criminality, between deliberate and willful deviance and deviance that cannot be helped. This keeps separate two massive jurisdictions. The willful transgressor becomes a ward of the criminal and prison system while those who are judged psychotic become wards of the mental health system.

Sometimes these issues are not clear-cut. Suppose we pick on Russia for the moment. It is repeatedly claimed that the Soviet government uses the diagnosis of insanity to incarcerate political dissidents. We make every effort to avoid doing this in the United States, but if a political dissidence is accompanied by bizarre behavior and life-styles, the diagnosis can have similar consequences in this country. Further, the use of diagnostic labels is not a tactic only of the right-wing in America. Over 500 American psychiatrists were willing to state, during the 1964 political campaign, that Barry Goldwater was psychotic.

2) *Circumvention of Cultural Conflicts.* There is another ambiguity about culpability and psychosis that is played out in law and in other institutions as well. The use of the psychotic label can circumvent certain serious conflicts in our cultural values.

Consider the example which is most evident in France, although it occurs more subtly in all Western nations. If a husband murders his wife and his defense claims that this is a crime of passion, the murderer is highly likely to be exonerated. There are various ways to interpret this extreme application of convenience. One of them is this: The right to kill an unfaithful spouse has been time-honored in some Western nations. It protects the sanctity of marriage, but it conflicts with law and our general horror of murder. So the passionate slayer faces us with a conflict of mores, one that we may be ambivalent about facing and resolving. Exoneration by a claim of passion maintains the ambiguity. Infidelity is a punishable offense.

3) *Exoneration of the Privileges.* A plea of mental instability can solve a conflict of interests and preserve the status of an important person as well. Foucault (1965) tells us an historic example. In the reign of Louis XIII a French aristocrat who was minister of finance was caught stealing from the treasury. This was probably not an unusual occurrence, but the fact that the story became generally known created a conflict. Under the emerging laws of France, a culprit had to be punished regardless of status. Since the offender was an aristocrat, there was another conflict, because aristocrats were deemed infallible. If they were found guilty, the law of infallibility could not be maintained.

The dilemma was solved as follows. The court physician declared the minister not responsible by reason of senility. This sort of diagnosis and explanation not only solved the dilemma of guilt and privilege, but also saved the privileged from the stigma of a diagnosis of insanity on functional or characterological grounds.

THE POSSIBILITY OF ALTERNATIVES

The gist of my argument is now shaping up. I am saying that our social institutions control psychotic episodes but tend to sustain the schizophrenic adaptation by continuing to support and foster dependent relationships. Other institutions in the society tend to do so by defining deviancy, predicting its course and making pragmatic uses of the deviation. But there are even larger loops to this picture of sustaining processes. The processes of labeling and shaping deviance begin in the child's life long before he or she even comes to the attention of our legal and psychiatric institutions.

I have already sketched this idea in Chapter 1. I will only review the premises very briefly to broaden the picture. The prevailing ideas and myths about schizophrenia and psychosis are known in some degree to every person in our society. Teachers, neighbors, relatives and parents label children and make predictions about their future. In schools a deficiency in learning may be visualized as a preschizophrenic deficit. Relatives liken an unusual child to historic figures or to relatives who have been hospitalized for psychosis. This lore is transmitted to the deviant child. This and a continuing pattern of special handling can shape the course of the schizophrenic adaptation.

We must ask about the possibility of alternative social approaches to the unusual child and the schizophrenic adult. I do not think alternatives will be easy to bring about because we have so much investment in the way we do things now. Further, I do not think we can even be clear about what these alternatives could be until we more clearly understand the neuropsychological arcs of these loops. I will simply mention two alternatives here and we will come back to them later.

First, I agree with Szasz that we do the schizophrenic person a disservice by thinking he has a disease. I think instead we must conceive of schizophrenia as a deficiency in cognitive and neural organization relative to the standards of a contemporary industrial society. At the same time, we cannot say that schizophrenia is *not* a disease, since clearly there are certain neurometabolic disorders which cause deviant behavior. On this account I think we must relinquish our ancient trichotomy of social, psychological and biological categories. We must conceive of a new category of genetic and acquired deviation. Later on I will say how this can be done.

Secondly, I think we must develop alternative procedures for dealing with infants and families where "high-risk" factors can be perceived. We must learn to teach schizophrenic people communicative skills and ways to organize cognition, in addition to employing drugs and insight therapies. These recommendations will also be discussed later.

3

Schizophrenia and

Family Experience

The person who will be schizophrenic begins life and usually grows up in a family, so many theories have evolved about how family experience sustains, augments or causes schizophrenia and psychosis. At first glance these theories seem quite disparate or even contradictory, but I think a broader view allows us to see that each is an accurate, but limited, view of the same picture.

In my view we have some consensus among clinicians about the nature of social relationships in families with schizophrenic members, in spite of apparent differences. There is, however, much more to a systems view of family than a network diagram of relationships. For one thing, there are quite different types of familial connection. Affiliative or symbiotic connections are increased in schizophrenia, but face-to-face interaction is markedly decreased. Furthermore, the family, in a systems view, is a broader field of activity than the interpersonal relationship. For instance, family interactions take place in a household of spatial-temporal order and the family is part of a larger extended network and tradition. These matters seem relevant to schizophrenia, too.

I will not try to tackle all family issues here. Two of them—the mother-child interaction and the transmission of schizophrenia—will be taken up in the next chapter.

POPULAR CLINICAL THEORIES OF THE "SCHIZOPHRENIC" FAMILY

Most popular theories on this subject embrace a description of the family relations or traits and at least an implied theory of how schizophrenia is handed down in the family. The most popular theories about family relationships can be grouped as follows: 1) theories of excessive interdependence between family members; 2) theories of family homeostasis or stalemated conflict; and 3) the "double-bind" theory. Transmission theories imply or state that parental traits are handed down by learning identification and/or genetic inheritance. I will briefly review these and then discuss how they may get together.

1) *Theories of Excessive Interdependency*

Two decades ago Mahler (1958; Mahler and La Perriere, 1965) described an excessive symbiosis between mother and child in instances which would result in schizophrenia. Today it is rather generally accepted that such mother-child ties are commonplace and often lifelong in schizophrenia. Other authors have described an overdependency of familial ties in other terms. Bowen (1960) makes the point in another sense in claiming that family members in schizophrenia lack self-differentiation or autonomous ego strength. This view reminds us of Jayne's view of the bicameral mind (see Chapter 1).

Wynne et al. (1958) saw the family attachments as somewhat less binding and genuine, so they speak of "pseudo-mutuality" in schizophrenic families. In any event, there is wide clinical consensus that strong dependent ties characterize the relationships of families with schizophrenic members. I shall soon argue that the matter is not quite this simple.

2) *Theories of Homeostasis and Stalemate*

The second set of popular theories holds that the members of the schizophrenic family—primarily the parents—are entropied in a stalemate or "homeostasis," so that no change or maturation is possible. In such theories the schizophrenic member is believed to somehow manifest or live out the inertia or stalemate.

By and large this group of theories is quite vague about the nature of the stasis and the mechanisms by which the stasis affects the schizophrenic member, but one recent theory of this type is excitingly more specific on this score. In the view of Palazzoli and her co-workers (1978), each parent in such families has always held an unshakable belief that he or she knows how the family should be. These views are irreconcilable but neither party will budge and an absolute stalemate results. These authors also offer concrete examples which could explain how a child comes to act bizarrely or autistically in such a standoff. In one case a child acted like a very old man. They deduced that this child was trying to replace a recently deceased grandfather who had formerly brought a measure of guidance to the family's life.

At first glance these two sets of theories seem oppositional. One postulates an over-identification among family members, while the other postulates a stasis of head-on disagreements. But I think this apparent irreconcilability stems from a failure of our theorists to attend to two important matters in family life: 1) They refer to relationships between some, *but not all*, family members, and 2) they neglect the stage of family evolution. Later on I will discuss what difference these perspectives make.

3) *The Double Bind Theory*

A hypothesis of Bateson, Jackson, Haley and Weakland (1956) seems to offer a very different sort of explanation of the family origins of schizophrenia. In this view the child who will be schizophrenic is subjected throughout childhood to a contradictory set of instructions. To obey one kind is to disobey the other. The child has no way to escape this mutually conflicting field of developmental forces.

In the view of these authors, the contradictions in experience make it impossible for the growing child to distinguish important sorts of social cues and cognitive distinctions. This inability, in double-bind theory, *is* schizophrenia.

The Summation of These Theories

These theories cover aspects of a dimension of the schizophrenic family; however, we can achieve a broader view if we place them in a larger perspective.

Assuming a stalemate in family development, we can account for it much as we do in the case of any ultra static system. Trends in one direction are offset by equal ones in an opposite direction. In cybernetic terms, any effect acts retroactively upon any causal behavior to prevent a directional change. So it is logical in the absence of any external intervention that a standoff of parental efforts, each enhanced by a "hubris" of determined effort, could be the mechanism of stasis, as Palazzoli et al. (1978) have said. How a stalemate leads to schizophrenia may be a much more complicated matter, which will be discussed in future chapters.

Now imagine that the parents who can achieve no accord in their marriage each gain allies in the family. Some of the children are close to and in agreement with mother, for example, while others and perhaps some other relatives as well join forces with the father. In such a case the family is divided into *two opposing coalitions*. In my own experience this configuration is a very common one at a certain stage in the life-history of a family.

If we consider that the members of opposing coalitions have and evince quite different viewpoints, we can bring theories of family stasis in line with double-bind theory. The members of one coalition may continuously bombard the growing child with one set of messages which are countermanded by those of the counterfaction. It is my view, published elsewhere in detail (Scheflen, 1978), that the conflict of interest often centers around the expectations of the family for their children. For example, one faction, often including the father and older siblings, pushes toward greater independence and cognitive mastery, while the other one, which often includes the mother, insists upon greater *dependency* for the child and on less progression toward maturation in general. Later we will see that this greater leniency and overprotection by the mother's coalition may rest upon a more realistic recognition of the deficiencies of the child who will become schizophrenic.

Whatever the details of this relationship, I think we can agree on the general proposition: A family of opposing coalitions will provide a field of contradictory propositions for a growing child.

How can we reconcile the view of opposition coalitions with the view of the schizophrenic family as a meshwork of overly dependent ties? First of all, I think that the difference is *in part* an artifact of observational scope. In some perspectives, those of child development, for instance, the only relative of the patient to receive much attention is the mother. If the observer looks only at the mother-child relationship, a marked symbiosis might be reported without attending to the fact that this symbiotic dyad is but one faction in the large family. That this dyad stands in opposition to other family members might be overlooked. Furthermore, in such a perspective it might never even occur to us that one reason for the tightness of the mother-child tie is the opposition of the other family members.

In the 1950s attention was paid to the role of the father, whereas only the mother's role had been previously attended. The concept of the "absent father" in the schizophrenic family gained considerable popularity in family therapy. This phase was usually figurative in family therapy circles, which dealt mainly with middle-class nuclear family units. The absent father lived at home but he was detached and remote from his wife and her disturbed child. He refused to attend family sessions, for instance. When one deals with poorer families or with residual post-divorce families, the father is often literally absent as well.

In my experience, the syndrome of the detached, uncaring father is especially common in the later stages of the schizophrenic evolution. The schizophrenic "child" is now an adolescent or an adult, sometimes with a history of several psychotic episodes. The mother has already devoted her life to controlling, protecting, even arguing with the patient. And this closed dyad has become virtually impermeable to the intervention of the therapist, father, or anyone else. In the advanced stage of family evolution the father has taken a peripheral stance toward this "gruesome twosome" (Scheflen, 1960b). At most he conceals his disapproval and adds his support to the mother. More likely, he detaches himself from the family and develops a life outside the home or leaves altogether. Some of the other children and relatives of the family also choose this way out.

The family now has a single coalition. Mother and patient, and sometimes another child or so, are members. But this picture of the family configuration does not necessarily mean that it was this way earlier when the patient was still a developing child. Unfortunately, we do not get a chance to examine many schizophrenogenic families before there is evident schizophrenia. However, we do see families early in the process, we can take histories of family configuration before there were schizophrenic manifestations, and we have reports of schizophrenic family configurations from cultures in which fathers are critically active participants in family affairs. The Italian rural families reported by Palazzoli et al. (1978) are cases in point. In my view, when we do get data about schizophrenic families earlier in their life-cycle, we find the picture of opposing coalition that I have mentioned above.

In this configuration the family is divided into two opposing camps. The opposition may be hostile and overt or ambivalent and covert. The opposition presents a field of double-binding instructions. Each member of the immediate household belongs to one of the coalitions and other relatives may also be members. Within each coalition the members are mutually dependent, often overly dependent in that coalition which includes the more protective parent and the child(ren) who will be schizophrenic. Theories of symbiosis and opposing coalition are not incompatible.

A Critique of These Theories

The popular theories point to the idea that a symbiotic relationship is common and somehow important in the schizophrenic family. But there is much our clinical writers have not told us. All in all, I think we must criticize our clinical literature on three major counts:

1) There are many abstractions *about* the symbiotic relationship, but we do not have much descriptive information about the actual behavior of symbiosis.

2) While family therapy claims a systems view of the family, most of the theories proposed offer only a social level view of how family members relate to each other in language. They say little about the organization of behavior in the schizophrenic household and about the boundaries and contexts of this organization.

3) Our pictures of the schizophrenic household are not adequately developmental. We do not know, for example, how schizophrenia is

transmitted or whether the mother-child symbiosis is merely a maternal response to a subtly deficient infant.

THE SYMBIOTIC FIELD IN SCHIZOPHRENIA

In my view, *a field of symbiotic behavior is a cardinal feature of the schizophrenogenic family*. So important is this feature that I think we must say all we can about it. But notice that I have spoken of a *field of behavior* rather than a relationship. I have thus shifted from a social view of partners in a relationship to a field or systems view of the actions and events. There are advantages in clarity to be gained this way. We can deal, for example, with the fact that participation in the field can change. We can even envision the possibility that the behavior we label symbiotic is carried out by only one family member. When we do this, we can explain autism more clearly.

What Does Symbiotic Behavior Look Like?

I shall begin by saying what the behavior we call "symbiotic" looks like. It has gross levels. For instance, we find that people invariably stay together in spite of the fact that they endlessly repudiate each other in words. But here I will try to describe the more micro-levels of the behavior we clinically call symbiotic. One sees such levels minute to minute in a family interview and we can record these minutes on audio-visual media for more careful inspection.

I have personally made detailed analyses of movies or videotapes of about 20 schizophrenic families, and I have examined several hundred others. Colleagues have done still many others. So we have quite an experience in these matters. However, since I have published only one instance in detail (1973), I will report here what I have observed and concluded.

Most of the families I have studied are working-class or middle-class white Anglo-Saxon or Jewish-American families with one or two members who have already been diagnosed as schizophrenic. I have studied some families of Black-American, Hispanic, British, French, Germanic, and other backgrounds. In my experience those family members who have not been labeled schizophrenic vary greatly along a spectrum from psychotic to quite social, successful, and happy.

I do not find any particular set of traits—ethnic, class, or personality traits—which seem to me to be characteristic of family members with schizophrenic relatives. Sometimes such relatives are obviously more psychotic than the identified patient—but only sometimes. *Yet I do find a regular deviation in the ways these family members relate to each other.*

In at least some subrelationships within the family *there is an unusually low degree of interaction and involvement and an unusually high degree of attachment or affiliation.* This deviation from the norms of Western culture is sometimes apparent in language, but sometimes it is denied or concealed. Family members may speak of having high degrees of interaction. They may vigorously assert their lack of interdependence or even their mutual hostility, so the verbal layer of familial affirmation may or may not show this picture of low involvement and high affiliation. Nevertheless, the picture almost invariably appears in the visible, non-linguistic modes of family communication.

The Dimension of Low Interaction

In Western societies people interact by turning toward each other and exchanging gazes, facial displays, words and sometimes touches. In such configurations the participants show varying degrees of "involvement." At one extreme, for instance, they sit at maximum distances from each other, show expressionless or deadpan faces, avoid holding gaze and say little or speak only in quite formal modes to each other. At the other extreme, there is maximum involvement, the partners sit or lean toward each other, their gaze exchanges are frequent or protracted, they speak in animated ways and gesticulate a great deal. We see this sort of involvement in a lively discussion, an animated flirtation or a heated (as opposed to a cold) argument.

In the relationships of the schizophrenic person—in or outside of the family—we rarely find high involvements and active interactions. To be sure, the family members may state the highest love, mutual concern or preoccupation with each other or they may argue interminably, but they do not do so in the heightened interactional mode I have described. Instead, they take maximum distances, avoid looking at each other, speak past each other in flat voices. Their faces and bodies are relatively immobile. And often they do not speak, look at each other, touch or even stay in the same face-to-face space. In sum, the degree of interactional involvement is extremely low.

We must take into account the role of cultural norms in such a generalization. As I said in Chapter 1, it is the norm to show relatively low involvement behavior in northern European cultures, while in some cultures, such as Southern Italian or traditional Eastern European Jewish, most exchanges are carried out in high degrees of interactional activity. There is much facial expression, animated speech, and touching even in a routine family exchange. These differences have been studied by anthropologists, for example, by Efron (1941) and Birdwhistell (1970) and are well known. I have also described them in a publication (1974), so my assertion about low face-to-face involvement in schizophrenia is made in respect to cultural norms. *In schizophrenic relations, involvement is low by any standards.*

This assertion fits well with the clinical observation that schizophrenic people are often withdrawn or autistic. But it seems to be in conflict with the view that schizophrenic family members are often in symbiotic relationships. This is not the case. Involvement and interaction are different dimensions of behavior than attachments of a symbiotic kind. I will now try to spell out this difference.

A Picture of High Affiliation

In contrast to this picture of relatively low face-to-face involvement, at least some members of a schizophrenic family have very high degrees of affiliative behavior. They are overly dependent upon each other by contemporary Western industrial standards as theories of differentiation and symbiosis have claimed. Here is what highly affiliative behavior looks like when observed directly.

Those highly affiliated members of the family share values and institutional beliefs. They are in common devout Catholics or rabid conservatives or dedicated romantics. They may love music in common or share a wish to be actors or artists. They may or may not verbalize these commonalities, but they *show* them in many modalities of behavior. They dress alike and wear their hair in the same fashion, for instance. In fact, there may be several factions in the same family and the members of each wear common colors and clothing styles. It is as if each faction had a uniform. For instance, members of one faction appear for the interview in suits and dresses, while the other faction appears in open shirts, jeans, or slacks. The members of one faction all will have some article of red clothing, while the others will all wear something blue.

The similarities of affiliation are also evident in posture and facial sets. The members of an affiliative coalition look sad together. They all move little and slump in their seats. If another family faction exists, its members will bear a different demeanor. For instance, they seem animated or hostile in common. Not only do the members of a symbiotic field share common modes, *but they also change these together.* When one member's face becomes placid, so do the faces of the others. All slump backward together one after the other or even at the same time. A moment later mother changes her facial expression and so does her son. It is as if they are wired to respond to the same common but hidden signal. They share moods as if by contagion.

We may not see expressional changes in the chronically psychotic members of a family. In such cases only an immobile flatness is evident, but this pattern will be shared much of the interview by that relative (or those relatives) who are clinically viewed as being symbiotic partners of the patient.

A commonness of bodily behavior is evident in the tempo of movement. Sometimes the symbiotic pair seems to engage in an endless ballet of movement. The faces, postures and arm positions change together—again and again—as if locked into the same score of a family dance.

In sum, the participants in a symbiotic field show little interaction with each other but they show high degrees of coalition—like members of a chorus, a dance team or a football squad. These co-actions include similarities in dress, color use, insignia, hairdo, posture, facial expression and gesture, and they are evidenced by a simultaneity of movement and change.

Certainly these co-features would lead a clinical observer to the opinion that such family members lacked autonomy or self-differentiation.

Membership in a Symbiotic Field

By defining a field of co-active and affiliative behavior we leave open the question of *who* shares such behavior. I think it is important to do this, for in fact the co-participants sometimes change in the life of the family.

There is a classical picture of the schizophrenogenic dyad—lifelong in duration. Mother and child, history tells us, have always been extraordinarily interdependent. Now, years later, they sit before us. The child, now an adult, is hospitalized for schizophrenic psychosis and the mother sits indulgently talking for the patient, chiding, protecting, acting like the mother of a small and untrustworthy child. Such a pair also shares the micro-behaviors of over-affiliation which I have just described. In such cases the members of the symbiotic field are mother and child and this membership will last until one of them dies.

The matter of membership is more complicated. For one thing, it can change almost from minute to minute. I recall a family session in which the mother and her schizophrenic son moved in the synchronous hypnotic way I have described for about a half an hour. Then the mother became angry and animated and from then on father and son shared the symbiotic behavior. Often one sees a mother move and act in this way when and only when she is with her schizophrenic child. When she is seen alone she shows a high degree of animation or even flirtatiousness. Our patients also vary in this dimension. In family interview they share a sombre dress, a flat affect, and a hypnotic mobility with the mother or father, but apart in a group session, for instance, they do not act in this field of behaving. *A person can move in and out of the symbiotic field.*

However, commonly these memberships are made much more complex. Multiple family members may act together in these ways. I recall an instance of a mother and four daughters who looked like peas in a pod and moved together like wired toys in a slow and lugubrious ballet. Sometimes father is a member of the coalition. Often three generations of family members share in it. Further, in some families there are two opposition coalitions, each of which shares behavior in its own field of highly affiliative behavior. These fields of affiliative behavior are not always low in interaction. Sometimes there is a high level of verbal argumentation. Sometimes the low affectivity is punctuated by episodes of violence. But ordinarily the prevailing mood or tone of the shared behavior is one of hypoactivity, dullness, low mobility and anhedonic affect.

An intervention can change it, too. I recall a family session conducted by Bowen (1977). Six family members moved in slow, listless synchrony while the parents told the family story. Halfway through the session Bowen created a joke with the most psychotic member of the family. This young lady immediately laughed, became animated and began to speak actively with the therapist. One by one each family member followed suit. The entire tone of the session radically changed, apparently by virtue of a joke which gave a totally different significance to the ceremonial event.

In my experience, an attentive intervention by some visitor or family member can sometimes accomplish a change like this for a while. When father is away, for instance, mother and the children fall into a flat, non-interactional hypomobile state until he returns. If so, the concept of the absent father takes on a greater significance. More comprehensively, we should say that the absence of anyone not caught in the symbiotic field is important in the care of the schizophrenic family.

Looked at in this way, we can come to some wider notions about the symbiotic relationship in schizophrenia. *It is a state of the family* —a state that seems sometimes mutable—a state that often involves the child who will later be judged "schizophrenic." What role a symbiotic membership has in schizophrenia will concern us again and again.

Opposition and the Death of the Family

We hope that the symbiotic coalition is opposed. The father-husband demands that his spouse be more than a protective mother.

Other children demand interaction and get it. Often an opposition of life-styles may develop. One side is invested in the dyadic protection of the growing child, while the other represents the demands for maturation. If those who oppose the symbiotic coalition drop the effort, the battle is lost. The remaining family members can fall into a shared symbiotic state. This very occurrence may play a critical role in the emergence of clinical schizophrenia.

Unfortunately, this very turn of events is likely to occur. It is built into the nature of the family. The closeness, the closed relationship of the symbiotic partners alienates the other family members one by one. They withdraw their active involvement, and the withdrawal provides the other loop in a vicious cycle for it tightens the symbiotic bond. Family life is increasingly dull. Father spends more and more time at work or he takes a mistress. Siblings grow up and leave home. Grandparents die. Fewer and fewer outsiders penetrate the invisible wall of symbiotic preoccupation.

The family grows smaller with age. Eventually only mother and the schizophrenic child, now an adult, still live in the household. There are no offspring to this wedlock. Ultimately that branch of the family dies out.

The Autistic Outcome

The symbiotic lock can be broken. Sometimes the mother of an obviously schizophrenic infant turns the child over to an institution. The young adult schizophrenic may leave home and insist upon living alone. Or the seriously psychotic member may be more or less permanently hospitalized. Since members of a symbiosis are notoriously unlikely to accept or find other partners, these divorces generally condemn the schizophrenic person to a chronic institutional state of psychosis. Such patients may relate to no one and become completely autistic.

In Chapter 4 I will have more to say about the various consequences of a rupture in the symbiotic relationship. But here I want to make a final point about the symbiotic mode of behaving. The autistic states of schizophrenia are characterized by the following forms of behavior: 1) The patient sits or stands in a relatively motionless, hypotonic state with some grimacing but with a small repertoire of facial expressions; 2) the patient hallucinates a partner or at least listens for hallucinations; and 3) the body or some bodily part is rocked in a rhythmically, oscillatory manner just as it is in synchrony with a partner when the symbiotic state is shared. In short, the behavior of autism is quite the same as the behavior of participating in a symbiotic field. The difference is made by the absence of a partner.

SOME OBSERVATIONS ON HOUSEHOLD ARRANGEMENTS

Unfortunately, clinicians garner their information about the schizophrenic family by listening to what family members say to and about each other in the clinician's office. Although I know of little systematic in-the-home data about the schizophrenic household, there are some observations which might be significant if they are frequent.

On Extended Family Relationships

The general reduction in household size over the last four centuries must be important in the issues we are discussing. There are fewer and fewer relatives to intervene in family stalemates and symbiotic dead-ends. There are also fewer and fewer adults to interact with, care for, and teach our children in the first five years of life. Many isolated nuclear family units join friend networks who supply some of the services and experiences of extended family life, but many isolated families do not replace their lost relatives and friends rarely intervene like family members. Our children, then, are relatively impoverished in social experience and information. Who teaches little girls to flirt like uncles used to do? And who offers us our first sex play like cousins used to do?

I think we can argue that the fewer relatives a household has, the greater is the likelihood that no effective intervention will occur in opposing coalitions or closed symbiotic relationships. Also, it seems to be the case that schizophrenic families are especially prone to close their frontiers to any intervention. Commonly, the mother is closely attached to her mother, but not to anyone else, and it seems to many clinicians that the fathers of these families also have either one close family tie or sometimes none at all. Then, once a deviation becomes apparent in the family, the doors are closed to all outsiders and the family presents a front of solidarity (Wynne et al., 1958).

I recently saw a mother and father with a psychotic son who was 25 years old. The boy had had a psychotic break at age 15, whereupon they withdrew him from high school. They lied to the school authorities that they were moving to another town. In the last ten years, ten relatives, neighbors, or other visitors had been in their house. They had endured ten years of severe psychosis in the family without even consulting a physician. They had never heard of antipsychotic drugs and considered the prognosis hopeless. In doing this they had emulated the father's parents who had managed the father's psychotic brother in this way.

Unrecognized Figures of Importance

When we ask the family about household members, they often fail to mention people of great importance to the patient. Sometimes a grandparent lives nearby and plays a strong part in the patient's upbringing. Sometimes a servant who was critical in the child's early years has long ago left the family and been forgotten. In short, people who are not nuclear family relatives can be important in the schizophrenogenesis and we do not even learn about them unless we inquire.

Here is an extreme example. A well-to-do family had 13 children raised in a huge suburban mansion. One child only, the seventh in the sibship order, became chronically schizophrenic. We could not ascertain any way in which this child had been treated differently until we made a home visit. We then learned that this child had always had a bedroom in a separate wing of the house. No other family members lived there but a total of four frankly psychotic boarders had shared this wing of the household with the child who became schizophrenic.

Orbits and Hidden Jurisdictions

In a family with a "schizoid" or overdependent child, one can often observe that this child never gets far from the mother. Family members may complain that this child always hangs around the mother. She may send him off to play with other children, but he is soon back with a complaint or a request. If mother insists on some interpersonal distance, this child "moves in an orbit" around her. He stays within earshot and hangs about where he can see his mother. Each party may be ultrasensitive to the whim or hurt of the other. A symbiotic partnership is in the making.

As such a child grows older, school and other social demands increase the social distance of the partners. In fact, maternal concern or emerging pride may lead the partners to a mutual avoidance, but they are always under mutual surveillance. They know each other's movements. They maintain an equidistance in the household and cross-check each other at frequent intervals. They grow fearful when they cannot hear each other's movements in the house. In the words of the late Dr. Samuel Wright (1965), the schizophrenic spends his life looking backward to where the parent ought to be. The slightly less dependent child may function well if he or she remains under the protective aegis of a parent and does not transgress its borders. Such a child can relate to those children the mother approves. He can go to those places the mother goes. He can learn from those teachers the mother endorses. And he can learn those ideas the mother holds, too. Such a child can make an exemplary school adjustment—within the protective aegis. Such a child does not suffer a psychotic panic away from mother unless he strays into places, values, and company which she or the family do not endorse.

Private Turfs and Field Dependency

Every child should have a territory in the household. At the least there is part of a bedroom with a bureau for prized possessions and a bit of wall space to hang special photos or insignia. Most children also have places elsewhere in the house and neighborhood. I think the existence and the privacy of these territories are especially important to those who are schizophrenic.

One reason is obvious to clinicians. The interpersonal relationships in schizophrenia are so stressful that a place of retreat is especially welcome. But I think there is another reason for the critical importance of such places. As the symbiotic ties become less and less accept-able, the psychotic-to-be relies more and more on impersonal objects. Some of the objects have been viewed as transitional in the develop-ment of object relations (Winnicott, 1952). In schizophrenia the transition may not be made. I do not, however, view the objects in a schizophrenic's private turf to be merely objects of fixation. In schizo-phrenia *they replace the actions of other people in maintaining cognitive organization and emotional modulation.* The objects con-sist of favorite sayings, poems, and passages, of photos, insignia and memorabilia. There are photos of faces, faces of people important to the schizophrenic person, faces which may later appear as hallucina-tions. And there are pictures of eyes. I would guess there are "always" pictures with prominent eyes.

These objects are, of course, symbols, as well as cues, cues about what to think and how to act. So the private habitat is probably analogous to the mother's aegis and maybe to participation in the symbiotic field. The schizophrenic person has now become field de-pendent. The field is personal, impersonal or both. Outside of these fields the schizophrenic can become psychotic and back within them he can sometimes achieve a reorganization. But I am getting ahead on my story, for dependency fields and psychosis will concern us in Chapter 4.

THE FAMILIAL TRANSMISSION OF SCHIZOPHRENIA

We have still to address an ongoing question. How is schizophrenia maintained or transmitted in the family?

I have already claimed that a culture of schizophrenic lore is passed down in common culture (see Chapters 1 and 2). Children are sometimes compared to psychotic predecessors, threatened with becoming psychotic or even unwittingly encouraged to identify with schizophrenic life adjustments.

Links like this do not in any sense explain how schizophrenia is transmitted. Probably at the most such behaviors shape the form and content of the psychosis. There are at least two other ways a family can shape schizophrenia.

The Transmission of Traits

In the 1950s an effort was made to understand the cultural transmission of schizophrenia by examining the traits of the parents of schizophrenic people. A great many postulates were made about such traits, especially those of the mothers (Lidz, 1973). These reports were sometimes contradictory. For example, some studies reported that mothers were domineering while others emphasized their passivity. On the whole, I think no consensus was achieved by such approaches. Currently, however, the concept of borderline schizophrenia is popular and from this perspective there is a measure of agreement. It is said that one or both parents of a schizophrenic offspring are often, but by no means always, "borderline" themselves. A popular hypothesis which is corollary to this view is the three-generational theory which holds that schizophrenic traits accrue and increase over generations in certain family members to become clinically manifest in some successive generation (Bowen, 1978a).

The studies of Wynne et al. (1977) and of Singer et al. (1978) distinguish cognitive "deficiencies" in schizophrenia which are in some measure shared by other family members. Such sharing may indicate that the children of parents with such cognitive deficits do not acquire adequate cognitive abilities in the course of maturation, though the possibility of a common genetic problem is not ruled out. So far theories of cognitive deficiency have suffered from two serious conceptual flaws. First, they do not adequately distinguish the use of bizarre explanations from other forms of cognitive deviation. Second, they attend only to problems in communication by the use of speech. Certainly many patients explain themselves by repeating favorite family theories of psychosis. In this sense family characteristics are reflected in the cognitive strangeness of schizophrenia.

On Family Supports for Being Schizophrenic

Sometimes the family profits from having a psychotic member and in this sense the schizophrenia is wittingly or unwittingly sustained. Here is a case in point.

The family consisted of two middle-class and middle-aged parents and two grown children. The son was a physician and the daughter had been labeled schizophrenic and had a history of many hospitalizations. When a clinician conducted a long series of family therapy sessions with these people, a consistent theme appeared in these sessions. Both parents and the brother repeatedly blamed the daughter for her problems and disavowed her insistently and repeatedly in spite of the therapist's efforts to alter their attitudes. This important dimension of the family experience required explanation.

It became increasingly apparent that the schizophrenic daughter and her physician brother were remarkably alike in many ways and all family members harbored the dread that the brother, too, would become psychotic. In fact, they had a secret theory, based on some actual incidents, that the brother would become psychotic if and when the sister improved. Presumably, then, she *had* improved markedly since her previous hospitalizations, but her family members kept denying this and emphasizing how psychotic she was. We had reason to suspect that these exaggerations had figured in some of her previous admissions. Further, we often witnessed evidences in family sessions which suggested that she was provoked to verbal violence by characteristic baiting statements from her parents. Her brother also underscored her isolation by repeatedly repudiating her and withdrawing from her. In this family the members had a stake in maintaining her psychotic state.

The Still Unanswered Question

We have still not asked the sixty-four dollar question. Factors which shape and sustain schizophrenia do not tell us enough. There are questions we have yet to address:

1) Does the symbiotic field sustain and foster schizophrenia or is it a parental adaptation to an already handicapped infant?

2) Behaviorally and genetically how is schizophrenia transmitted or initiated?

4

Dyadic Interaction
in Schizophrenia

Failures in social adjustment tend to heighten the schizophrenic person's reliance on the dyadic partner in the family symbiosis, but this dyadic relationship is interactionally impoverished. The fact of the matter is that most *schizophrenic people are deviant and unaccomplished in the behavior of face-to-face interaction and they are often disinclined to make the effort to interact.*

We can observe this difficulty in any social encounter and any dyadic relationship in schizophrenia, including those of the family. In fact, there is some evidence that a subtle deficiency in interaction has characterized the mother-child relationship from the earlier days of life. If so, we have a critical clue for understanding the origins and transmission of schizophrenia.

SOCIAL ADJUSTMENTS IN SCHIZOPHRENIA

When we look backward at the pre-psychotic social adjustment of our schizophrenic patients, we usually find problems at each stage of life. Let us review some of the commoner types of problem.

The Preschool Period

Many of the parents of schizophrenics tell us that this child was always different—different from their other babies or different from

53

their expectations. They are hard pressed to find definitive words for the deviance. He seemed inert, passive, inattentive, we are sometimes told. Some mothers report a lack of warmth or smiling response. Some say the child would scream when left alone or whenever anyone tried to pick it up. Sometimes there were feeding problems and colic. Some mothers put the problem with their infants in another way, remembering things they seemed unable to do for that particular child, e.g., "I never seemed to hold him." One mother told me that she could not touch this particular child and did not know why. Dr. Jane Ferber recently showed me with a number of videotapes that an autistic child is almost impossible to pick up for it becomes either totally flaccid or extremely rigid whenever its mother makes the attempt (Yorberg et al., 1978).

Some children are so out of contact that they are diagnosed autistic in the first or second year of life, but in those who do not appear schizophrenic until later life a problem of contact is not obvious or describable. However, there are often childhood problems, such as an unwillingness to be left alone or an avoidance reaction to relatives other than mother. Such children may also be slow to smile, sit up and speak. In later childhood they show attacks of panic with illusions or delusions which are attributed to physical illness or extraordinary stress. Tachetoma (1977) claims that all schizophrenic adults have had unrecognized episodes of childhood psychosis.

The School Period

Many children who will be schizophrenic are alleged to have school phobias. Once in school they tend to be underachievers. Teachers describe them as inattentive, poorly motivated and unwilling to participate in class. Sometimes the school grades, like the intelligence tests, showed "scatter." There is marked ability in some particular subjects, with poor grades in others. The schizophrenic student is not usually regarded as lacking in intelligence.

It is usually said that the schizophrenic student was not popular. He or she did not make many friends. Girls commonly are said to have been passive and overcompliant to authority, while boys are more often passively defiant or uncooperative (Mednick and Schulsinger, 1972). There was usually not much participation in athletics, drama, school dances or other group activities. In the more marked instances, the child went to school, participated as little as possible, and rushed home to solitude or family life as soon as the school day ended.

But there are three other types of school adjustments which we often hear about in those who will later be deemed schizophrenic. In one of these the child is persistently and desperately unsocial and antisocial. He defies authority, refuses help from everyone, and loudly defends the role of loner. Such children may end up with the diagnosis of antisocial character and accumulate records of drug abuse, sexual promiscuity, crime, and violence. They are "touchy." They recoil at any advance, however well meaning. Later on they may bear the diagnosis of "paranoid schizophrenia."

Another pre-psychotic type is the impeccably proper and hypermoral student with strong attachments to the family and to some overriding ideology—fundamentalist Christianity, for instance. Such children may have exemplary school records and are well liked by authoritarian figures. They may even achieve some popularity if they do not proselytize their schoolmates or act in a superior manner. But we find a problem if we inquire very closely. These pre-schizophrenic children talk at and to other people. They perform, but they do not interact or engage or share in social processes.

There is a third sort of schizophrenic-form school adjustment. Children of this kind form serious closed dyadic relationships with one other person at a time. While such a relationship lasts, it is all important. Other contacts are avoided. Great jealousies surround the relationship if the partner forms other attachments. The dyadic partners stand alone against the rest of their universe. Then an overly devastating fight can occur, leading to great despair and loneliness and perhaps to a tragic end, when one partner tries to establish some distance. Less dreadfully, this dyad is replaced by another and then maybe another. *It can be said that the schizophrenic person tends to live either in one-to-one or in one-to-none relationships.*

The Post-School Adjustment

Most school children who will become schizophrenic drop out or graduate and go on to college or employment while still living at home. Some go away to college, to military service, to better work opportunities or they just take off. A large percentage of those who are schizophrenic will become obviously psychotic in a few months if they leave home at this point. This issue will concern us in Chapter 5. Those who stay at home may make a college or work adjustment not unlike that of their high school period. They tend to be under-achievers, avoiding most group activities. Those who are more "schizoid" may only attend necessary work or school activities and spend the rest of their time at home in their bedrooms. Some continue an active antisocial career or take up an ideology which they may advocate in an antisocial way. Commonly, schizophrenic people do not complete educational and vocational undertakings and when they do they tend to accept employment much below their qualifications.

Some schizophrenic and borderline people marry. In some cases, marriage is accomplished because a more active and socially competent partner takes leadership in the relationship and comes to replace the schizophrenic person's partner in a symbiotic relationship. In other instances, both partners are dependent so the marriage is supported by the parents of one of the partners. Yet, in all fairness, some people who develop schizophrenic psychosis do seem to have had quite adequate marital and parental adjustments prior to the psychosis.

In sum, many people who develop a schizophrenic psychosis have a pre-psychotic history of social failure and "schizoid" traits. Others seem to have functioned adequately as long as they lived at home and had the support of a parent or a family. There are also patients who seem to have made an adequate adjustment before the onset of psychosis. These people challenge our view of the lifelong duration of the schizophrenic state.

SOCIAL WITHDRAWAL AND SOCIAL INEPTITUDE

The commonest pre-psychotic picture is that of a person who is more or less socially withdrawn from all other people or from all other people except maybe the mother, another relative or possibly one peer. Because of this we commonly say that the pre-psychotic or schizophrenic person is withdrawn from most relationships but symbiotic in one or two.

There is a vast literature on the psychology of this withdrawal (Fromm-Reichmann, 1950; Searles, 1955; Arieti, 1974; Kernberg, 1968). In psychodynamic perspective, various reasons or motives for withdrawal are cited. For example, the schizophrenic person often distrusts other people and distrust his own motives and behaviors. In other ascriptions, the low self-esteem and fear of failure are stressed, though some schizophrenic people have a grandiose disdain for other people. Affects are cited as explanations of the withdrawal in some psychodynamic accounts. The patient is too hostile to relate, for example. Or in paranoid states it is often alleged that the patient's homosexual anxieties interfere with relationships. All in all, dozens of motivational and affective ascriptions are commonly postulated to explain the social withdrawal.

There is no doubt that such preoccupations and affects attend the schizophrenic withdrawal, but there is a serious problem in giving them *the* causative role in the inadequate social connectedness of schizophrenia. In the first place, the psychological preoccupations and the social failures have a cyclic relationship. Failure engenders a fear of failure and a negativity about social attachments, which in turn augment an inadequacy of social adjustment. The schizophrenic person does not merely think or feel he or she is socially inept; there is a long history to prove it.

But there is even more to the story. The psychology of withdrawal is also sustained within loops at the social level. The child or adult who is caught in a close and exclusive dyad is not free to form social relationships with anyone else. This loop of seclusiveness also involves the cognitive abilities and the behavior of the pre-psychotic person. Outside the supportive dyad such a person may lack the cognitive ability to sustain a role in social interactions. This problem will concern us in Part II of this volume. Furthermore, the person with schizophrenic problems is unaccomplished in the microbehavior of social interaction. This point I will take up next, but I want first to assert strongly that *we cannot explain schizophrenic withdrawal or social difficulties solely by describing the patient's feelings and thoughts about self and others.* The patient's and the family's explanations do not necessarily encompass a view of the social and neurobehavioral connections of this difficulty. They are not adequate informants.

I am not questioning the validity of our many reports of the psychology of alienation and antisocial behavior. I have no doubt that such attitudes and affects are one crucial arc in the problem. But I am insisting that we consider others as well.

THE INTERACTIONAL PROBLEM IN SCHIZOPHRENIA

A serious deviance underlies these relational problems in schizophrenia. The schizophrenic person has very real problems in interactional behavior. Let me describe and illustrate these with some direct observational data, which can be seen on any close observation of interactional participation, especially if one takes time to record such interactions on movies or videotape for careful replay.

Bear in mind that, in watching such occurrences, we watch motor behavior and examine its patternment in a relationship. In such an approach we do not jump to inferences about what the participants are thinking or feeling.

Interaction in the Hospital Setting

On the hospital ward the active psychotic patient can be a notorious nuisance. In one way of saying it, his manners are atrocious. He follows the staff members with endless demands. He haunts the nursing station, demanding attention. The other patients may be treated with contemptuous avoidance, but when any staff members convene for a conversation this patient barges right into the group. He does not await even the acknowledgment of a glance before interrupting with a demand. He steps between the nurse and the psychiatrist, turns his back on one of them and stands eyeball to eyeball with the other one to verbalize a demand. There is an utter disregard of the simplest rules of human territoriality.

"But," you may say, "he is crazy. What do you expect?" Let's look at it in another way. Craziness *is* a failure (among other things) to obey the rules of territoriality and decorum. Also, observe the same patient months later when he is no longer considered psychotic and an ameliorated form of the same transgressions is detectable. Now he sits quietly in a group therapy session, but he invades other people's space with his gaze and he interrupts before the others have finished speaking. Manners are a form of social competence. Some schizophrenic people, often the paranoid ones, automatically and habitually fail to master them.

Most of the patients on the ward have the opposite trouble. Watch them closely at a ward session. Most sit languidly and hypotonically with no trace of the bodily alertion one normally supplies to a group endeavor. The faces are generally flat. They hold expressions to be sure—anger, depression, or boredom, for example—*but these do not change much*. They are especially unlikely to change in tune with the expressions of others in the group. The participants do not face each other or even hold glances very often. In fact, they do not react to each other at all or in the ways we might expect. One overreacts and reacts too quickly. Another responds after an interminable pause. The timing is very off—like a very bad orchestra.

Some deviances in communicative behavior are much subtler than these. Gaze is an example. The schizophrenic person can look at you but focus the eyes a foot beyond you. He seems to be looking through and beyond; conversely, the gaze is focused in front of the conversational partner. Many schizophrenic people also invariably avoid gaze contact. A few gaze fixedly and make you most uncomfortable. The pupils are often overly dilated or overly constricted—a deviance which we know now is significant in warmth and rapport or coldness and distance.

Schizophrenic people are also characteristically deficient in greeting behavior. Not only do they fail to say hello, but they make no acknowledgment of your arrival with gaze, smile, or a display of the palm of the hand. Some schizophrenic people have greeting behavior, but it is deviant. The hello is overly loud, for example. The glance of recognition is a stare. However, even in schizophrenics who show greeting behavior, the display of the palm is still often absent, even though this display appears in greeting around the world. In fact, it is noteworthy that schizophrenic people rarely show the palm of the hand in any encounter. This, in itself, is unusual; for that matter schizophrenic people tend not to use the hands very much to gesture or to touch.

All in all, schizophrenic people tend not to use the most funda- mental linking behaviors of human interaction, i.e., facing, gaze, eye convergence, voice projection, palm displays and touch. A schizo- phrenic person who uses these behaviors is unusual or deviant— deviant by the norms of his own particular culture. We can observe gross evidences in the mental hospital, but in my experience the deviations and absences are lifelong in at least many patients.

There is a huge literature in the basic sciences of communication on nonlanguage behaviors and their social significance (Birdwhistell, 1970; Kendon, 1977; Scheflen, 1972, 1974). Clinicians not familiar with the literature may not notice these deviations in a conscious way or they may abstract them as "symptoms." Those unversed in this subject often do not realize the importance of gaze and other micro- acts in forming and maintaining relationships. To the communica- tional scientists an inability to perform these repertoires adequately is a serious matter, for such deviations and inadequacies make it almost impossible to engage in normal social discourse.

Interactional Disabilities in Highly Motivated Patients

In most phases of schizophrenia the patient is anxious to avoid social engagement. This avoidance obscures the fact that schizo- phrenic people are also unable to participate with competence in social interaction. There is, however, a stage in schizophrenia when some patients are highly motivated to interact and to learn how to do so. In my experience this occurs in young adult schizophrenics who are recovering from a psychotic episode in an institution which has programs in socialization.

As a matter of fact, I have occasionally worked with young staff members in institutions where we actually coached many patients like this in gaze, touch and other modalities of interpersonal contact. *When one sees such patients desperately trying to master such behav- iors, the schizophrenic problems in social participation become vividly apparent.*

Let me describe some examples. A young woman was painfully

aware that she could not look directly into the face of another person. When she tried to do so, her gaze became almost uncontrollable. When she tried to force herself with great conscious effort, her eyes would go into a marked side-to-side clonic movement.

It was noticed that a young man always concealed his right hand behind his back in any conversation or group activity. This was pointed out and it was explained to him that his hands were critical for cueing in social interaction. The palm is not only critical in greeting and courtships but in gaining the attention of others in order to speak during a conversation (Kendon and Ferber, 1975). Apprised of these matters, the young patient diligently began to learn about using his hands in social interaction, but he was unable at first to control the arm. We then discovered that he was also fearful of touching anyone with his right hand. An enterprising young therapist taught the patient to touch with this arm and then he was able to use it (rather clumsily) in gesticulation.

These experiences are quite like those of the "forced hugging" therapists (Yorberg et al., 1978). These people force mother and autistic children to hold each other. At first both mother and child resist the procedure with vigor but when forced to do so they rather quickly learn and gradually become accomplished at it. Yet, until the procedure was tried, we did not realize either the depth of the resistance or the simple fact that these mothers did not know how to hold a child. Concomitantly, of course, these children did not know how to be held. This issue will concern us again later.

It is now clear that the schizophrenic person's failure to engage in social interaction is both a resistance and a lack of ability. Obviously, these factors are mutually causative, but if we do not recognize that schizophrenic people do not know how to enact the social order, it will not occur to us to teach them (Scheflen, 1976).

The social inability is not simply a lack of proficiency in touch, gaze, palm use and the other ABC's of social discourse. It even more clearly is an inability to participate in the more complex activities of human engagement. Schizophrenic people are characteristically unskilled at conversation, courtship and confrontation, for example. To be incompetent in any of these complex sequential activities constitutes a handicap of serious proportions.

Consider deviations in courtship patterns. The usual picture in schizophrenia is a virtual absence of any courting behavior at all—even if there is sexual behavior. In fact, the behavior of most schizophrenic people could be regarded as the converse of a courting demeanor. In courtship, gaze is met and sometimes held. In schizophrenia, gaze is avoided or in some paranoid forms it consists of a fixed and penetrating stare. In courtship, the participants preen themselves. They stroke their hair, faces, or limbs, for instance, and women flash their open palms. The schizophrenic person tends not to use the hands in social relationship. In courtship, the bodies of the partners are held erectly and in high forms. The head is erect; the breasts or the chest, as well as, perhaps, the pelvis and the legs, are displayed. The schizophrenic's trunk sags in a hypotonic, almost immobile way; his head hangs; his face it flat, almost immobile. The signs of high attention and interest essential in courtship are usually missing in schizophrenia.

When courtship does occur in schizophrenia, it is marked or extreme. As in all other dimensions, schizophrenic courting is a state of extremes. Let me describe the picture of hypercourting which occasionally occurs in schizophrenia—usually accompanying a paranoid form of cognition. In these less usual examples, the body is highly tonic and mobile as if ready to spring into overmobility. The eyes are alive. The picture is one of immensely brightened charisma. In women like this there are endless displays of the breasts and palms. The hands and fingers are moved in slow writhings and graceful circles. This is the behavior which the professional model cultivates so carefully and turns on for the camera. But a schizophrenic person with such courtship behavior has no such control. The courting displays go on almost interminably. Often the patient does not even know or understand the significance of his or her behavior. The charismatic paranoid is at first surprised that he can recruit a cult following. The beautiful and highly courting young woman is surprised at receiving sexual advances she has not knowingly solicited. She turns in fear from other people or sometimes passively complies and becomes involved in promiscuity or prostitution without any sexual enjoyment.

There is a serious problem here in the relationship of motor behavior and consciousness. There is also a problem in understanding the social significance of behavioral cues. This is one aspect of the logical types problem discussed by Bateson et al. (1956; see Scheflen, 1978), in double-bind theory. The schizophrenic has not mastered the basic repertoires of his cultural heritage, and there is a failure to distinguish patterns of a similar kind.

One must wonder about the role of such uncertainties in the genesis of paranoid ideas. I think nothing generates suspiciousness more than a continuing ambiguity. Imagine what it must be like to grow up never knowing the intent of those who approach us. To make matters worse, a person so confused about interactional patterns does not understand what his behavior means to other people either. Maybe this is why so many schizophrenic people become so frozen and immobile. If any movement is mysterious in implication, it becomes risky to move and safer to hold still.

Schizophrenic participation in confrontation is deviant, too. As in courtship, the deviance errs in both directions, i.e., most schizophrenics avoid confrontations while a few engage in them almost endlessly. Those of the first group go to any lengths to avoid the slightest arguments. They show the same remote, inarticulate and hypotonic forms of non-participation that they show in a conversation or courtship. The more aggressive, paranoid people are contentious in language. They invade other people's space. Jaw and chest are set in an almost continuous jut. Vision is piercing and challenging.

Certainly the social behavior of schizophrenia can be attributed to motives and affects. It obeys in part the psychodynamics of situation and personality, but for each patient there are persistent stereotypical and lifelong patterns too. *One aspect of this is a failure of experience.* Appropriate forms and appropriate degrees of modulation have not been achieved. A failure to distinguish rapport from seduction has its paranoid counterpart in a failure to distinguish helpful criticism from cold destructive anger. The paranoid often cannot make such distinctions about the behavior of others, nor does his own behavior allow others to be sure whether he is violent. In short, schizophrenia is, among other things, an inadequacy of social experience.

INTERACTIONAL DEVIANCE IN THE
SCHIZOPHRENIC-MOTHER DYAD

High Symbiosis and Low Interaction

There is one other situation we should observe in order to visualize the schizophrenic problem in interaction. In many instances mother and patient sit together in the same room with almost no interaction at all. They do not speak to each other unless a third party (such as a family therapist) stirs up a point of controversy or special interest. If the partners do speak to each other, they often do so without looking at each other. Mother and son many each act as if the other one were not present. I recall a family session in which a father, a mother and a grown son actively discussed family problems for two hours. The mother knitted throughout the session. In spite of several heated exchanges with her son, at no point in the two hours did she even glance up from her knitting to look at him.

I think this story typifies the interaction relationship of the mother-schizophrenic dyad. There are high degrees of mutual dependency and affiliative behavior, *but a remarkable absence of the behaviors of direct, face-to-face interaction, of facing, looking, gesticulation and touching.*

As I said in Chapter 3, the mother of these symbiotic dyads may or may not act differently in other relationships. Occasionally, for instance, one observes a mother who shows quite usual, even animated, interactional behavior in other relationships. Yet when she is with her schizophrenic offspring she adopts the low interactional mode I have been describing. If one interviews such mothers, one finds they may be well aware of this. Some say, "I act that way with Johnny (or Mary) in order to fit in with his (her) way." One mother told me that whenever she used interactive behavior with her schizophrenic son he became very anxious. She said she had learned to tone down and slow up her behavior with her son years before when he was a baby in order to achieve a measure of comfortable contact. In such instances, we can suspect that the mother's behavior is an accommodation, an attempt to share a mutually tolerable mode of relatedness.

However, in other cases we can observe that the mother *acts the same way with everyone.* She does not exchange gaze, touch, or face-to-face activity with her husband, her other children or her parents, and she may tell us that her marriage and her life are deficient in sexuality, conversation, and even in argumentation. Such mothers appear to share their schizophrenic child's interactional deficiency and may also share the cognitive and adjustment problem of the more schizophrenic members. They are often judged to be "borderline" schizophrenic and such hypotonic, immobile, flat people seem to be the ones clinicians judge to be "emotionally weak." Since this interactional deficit is seen in successive generations, some family therapists speak of a three-generational transmission of "emotional weakness" (Bowen 1978a).

I think we do better to use somewhat different terms, for observations such as "emotional" do not capture a vision of just what the deficiencies are. Also, we will have to deal later with the mechanisms by which these interactional modes are transmitted. For the moment I prefer to say that the interactional deficiency (often called "emotional") is shared in some families. In others it seems that the family has evolved a special mode for dealing with a child who interactionally is deficient *on some other basis.*

The Maternal-Neonatal Relation in Schizophrenia

There are some indications that this interactional problem may originate very early in the life of the child.

The infant who will become schizophrenic is not ordinarily a victim of abuse or gross neglect, but there seems to be a specific subtle problem in establishing the mother-infant relationship. We have a few filmed documents which suggest what this problem is in the case of autistic children.

Masse (1973) reports an instance in which the father had made home movies of the mother-infant interaction from the time of birth until the child was clearly autistic and socially withdrawn. A communicational analysis of this film showed that the mother had always prevented this infant from making eye contact with her. She also avoided touching it with the palms of her hands. Birdwhistell (1970) also reported a film analysis of a mother who avoided gaze and tactile contact with her new infant. This mother already had an older child who was autistic. Stern (1974) filmed the interaction of a mother who had identical twins. The mother and the infant who was judged normal employed a usual pattern of mutual gaze. The other twin was diagnosed as autistic in the first year of life. This child and the mother showed a persisting pattern of mutual gaze avoidance. In another publication (Scheflen, 1978), I have described other such instances and given more details about this deviant mother-infant interaction.

In cases of marked autism, the child does not relate to the mother at all. Such children do not gaze at, touch or otherwise attend to other people. Condon (1975) has shown that autistic infants move in relation to outside noises instead of following the mother's speech or body. There is a lack of smiling, inadequate speech and delayed psychomotor development. It seems likely that children with a less serious problem do not become obviously autistic and are not perceived as clinically abnormal. Yet they show problems of gaze, smiling and crying. Some scream when they are left alone. Others scream when they are held. Some are so flaccid or hypertonic that it is difficult to pick them up or hold them (Ferber, 1978).

Infants with difficulties like this may elicit protective responses and the special attention of the mother or of some other older person. In some of these relationships, the child follows the partner about, clings, and refuses to relate to anyone else. The mother (or mother surrogate) may devote herself to this child in an exclusive way. A symbiotic relationship forms.

As I have previously claimed, the symbiotic pair is increasingly alienated from other family members, and a vicious cycle is established. The mother's preoccupation with the child separates her from the others and their alienation turns the mother and child back to their dependency on each other. As the child gets older, the symbiotic bond is more and more acceptable and constraining. The partners blame each other, argue and avoid each other. Eventually there is little interaction between the schizoid child and its mother and both of these partners have little to say or do with other family members. The bond is now covert.

Part II

The Schizophrenic Person: Organismic Levels in Psychosis and Schizophrenia

In Part I, I designated four social levels of organization and sketched a view of concepts and observations at each of these levels of perspective. In doing this I simply ignored certain hypothetical problems about criteria and sublevels. This oversimplification and a relatively small literature on the sociology of psychosis and schizophrenia made it possible to be relatively brief. However, when we move on to examine schizophrenia at organismic levels, we cannot get by so easily. We encounter a vast literature and an incredible degree of conflict and confusion.

There are at least three sources of this diversity and confusion. First of all, schizophrenia is not a simple syndrome. In classical terms there are at least five distinctly different "subtypes." I will deal in this volume with the pleomorphism of the organismic picture by delineating four states or stages of psychosis and two states of schizophrenia in which there is no obvious psychosis. In addition, the delineation of organismic levels is not simple or agreed upon even within the perspectives of general systems theory; analogous perspectives in the clinical sciences are even more muddled by dichotomies such as psychodynamic vs. physiological, or emotional vs. cognitive.

To make matters worse, the organismic phenomena of psychosis and schizophrenia have been approached from the vantage point of two vastly different paradigms: the biological and the psychological. Each of these paradigms has splintered into a variety of very different disciplines, and each viewpoint has been employed to study schizophrenic people. Further, each of these approaches studies different sorts of patients and uses different methods and observational foci. In the biological paradigm the behavior patterns of schizophrenia are abstracted as symptoms of disease, while in the psychological framework they are abstracted as deviations in ego functioning, cognition or emotionality. The actual behavior of the psychotic person is rarely even described, so it is difficult to make inferences about suborganismic processes. Needless to say, each approach has its own private language. All in all, then, we have a huge literature of conflicting findings, and we are never sure that the various investigators are even dealing with the same kind of processes or occurrences.

THE TASK AND AGENDA

There are two traditional ways of dealing with this vast confusion. In most books and review articles, the author simply lists the many orientations and summarizes the findings with little or no synthesis attempted. In clinical practice, the confusion is usually avoided in another way. The clinician takes a position within one of the established doctrines; having the revelations of a "real truth," he ignores all contradictory findings and alternative points of view.

However, we are attempting in this book to present a unified picture of the states and processes of schizophrenia at each level. So there is no escaping the task: We must examine our frames of reference, make our existing data more consonant and hammer out a more unified view.

Here is the agenda I will use to do this. I will define the organismic view at the beginning of Chapter 5 and the suborganismic level of organ systems or physiological systems in Chapter 6. I will consider the other conceptual problems as they arise.

In Chapter 5 I will describe body states and emotionality in various forms of psychosis. This will allow us to say something about autonomic, extrapyramidal, corebrain and neuro-hormonal activities. In Chapter 6 I will review what we know or can infer about physiological subsystems, including those of the central nervous system. In order to make inferences about neural integration in the central nervous system, we shall make use of the classical approaches to psychoanalytic and cognitive psychology, as well as those of the newer neurophysiological studies. When we do this, we can integrate psychological and neurophysiological views to gain a picture of the "neuropsychology" of schizophrenia and the degrees of neural disorganization which characterize each of its psychotic stages.

Collectively, the two chapters of Part II give us a view of the schizophrenic dysfunction described in organismic terms. This dysfunction will make more sense to us as we go on in Part III to examine the problems of synaptic transmission and the metabolism of neurotransmitters in the neuronal fields of the central nervous system.

5

Bodily and Physiological States in Schizophrenia

In this volume we are moving our focus one level at a time from a view of society to a view of molecular processes. We are now at the level of analysis at which we must visualize one organism or person at a time. In general systems theory, this level is often termed the organismic level.

A focus on the individual is commonplace in psychology and psychiatry, but often the concept is reduced to a view of individual differences or personality profiles. The systems concept at the organismic level demands a much more comprehensive view of the human organism. It not only includes aspects of motor behavior and inferences about needs, but also encompasses the picture of integrated bodily or physiological states. The human organism experiences multiple organismic states which change with environmental events and with the activities of the physiological and metabolic subsystems.

It is difficult for us to conceptualize this degree of complexity. In theory we would have to have a simultaneous readout of every physiological subsystem to assay any organismic state, and we would have to have a way to visualize the integration of all these data and to relate them to context. We could not do this adequately with our present knowledge, even if we had a battery of labs and computers. We certainly cannot do so in a clinical interview. So we must make certain approximations. We can observe certain features of the subject's or client's behavior that allow us an index of the more complicated organismic condition. In this chapter I will use three sorts of approximations: indices of health, well-being and nutrition; bodily states and activity levels which we attribute to involuntary neural activity; and the motor behavior of schizophrenia.

Using such indices represents a reduction of the complexity of organismic states, so this method does not do justice to the complexity of schizophrenic states. Yet it is preferable on several grounds to the kinds of reduction we have classically made in studies of schizophrenia. In these classical reductions, we have interpreted the organismic phenomena of psychosis and schizophrenia as merely a reaction to some situation or an expression of some disease or mentalistic aberration. Worse yet, we have jumped to these assumptions *before* we have even described our observations. As a consequence, we have not bothered to describe the behavior of schizophrenia since the early part of the twentieth century.

We have paid heavily for this omission. When we try to say what schizophrenia is, we can only toss out doctrinal clichés such as "ego weakness," "cognitive deficit," or "genetic disease." So we must now backtrack and do our scientific homework. We must say what observations we can make about psychosis and schizophrenia at the organismic level. When we have done so, we will be in a much better position to make inferences about psychological and neural processes.

In this chapter I will first describe relatively persistent bodily states in schizophrenia. Then I will define the observational basis of the clinical concepts of emotionality. At the end of the chapter, I will begin to distinguish four degrees of disorganization in schizophrenic psychosis.

BODILY STATES IN SCHIZOPHRENIA

Think about the situations in which we, as clinicians, make observations about the organismic states of a schizophrenic person. Sometimes we watch the patient sitting in a hospital ward. On other occasions the patient is sitting across from us in an interview. At times certain relatives may be included, and we can see the patient in a setting of family relationships. In any of these situations, we cannot see or hear neural processes, cognition or emotion. We can only infer them. What we observe are features of appearance, bodily states and the actions of speech and movement.

Sometimes the deviations in appearance and bodily state are so characteristic and so obvious that we can make the diagnosis of schizophrenia at a glance. Sometimes they are less evident, and their existence is brought out only by careful observation, a case history and some probing queries. Occasionally, we do not observe schizophrenic deviations at all in the first encounter, and it is only in the course of therapy that they become apparent to us.

In any event, there are no laboratory tests to make the diagnosis for us. Also, some experienced schizophrenic patients who fear hospitalization or treatment can give a very good verbal account of themselves. If we are not to belatedly realize we have overlooked a schizophrenic problem, it is important that we watch bodily sets, facial reactions and patterns of behavior instead of becoming too engrossed in interpreting *what* the patient says. A close relative will probably tell us, "He sometimes acts strangely, and he just doesn't look right." We are to figure out what is strange and what is not right. Suppose then that we look at four dimensions of bodily states.

Signs of Health and Nutrition

Some schizophrenic people present a picture of robust health and high vitality. Young paranoid types in their first episode of manifest psychosis are an example. It hardly occurs to us to raise questions about their health or nutrition. But even in these instances we can observe a subtle deviation. There is an excessive brightness of the eyes, and the appearance of vitality begins to take shape as a poorly controlled restlessness and a marked increase in muscular tonus and arousal.

A large number of schizophrenic patients impress us from the start as lacking in health or nutrition. Sometimes they show signs of a specific physiological disturbance. There is a vague impression of hyperthyroidism in some acutely psychotic or paranoid patients and some passive, chronically psychotic people look as if they suffer from hypothyroidism. Some exhausted and weak patients make us think of adrenal insufficiency. We wonder if they are suffering from avitaminosis. Although adrenal insufficiency is not clinically evident in most schizophrenic patients, it may play a role in the exhausted and depressive states which often follow an acute psychosis in which the patient is often sleepless, overactive and in panic for days or sometimes weeks.

In former decades when exhausting physical treatments such as insulin coma therapy or massive electroshock were routinely administered, deaths did occur from adrenal exhaustion. Possibly this occurrence indicated a relative adrenal insufficiency related to the psychosis. In the 1950s observations like this led some theorists to postulate that adrenal disorders were the cause of schizophrenia.

While the pituitary-adrenal pathways are not clearly abnormal in most instances of schizophrenia, there are often abnormalities of the other neuro-hormonal pathways. Disorders of the infundibular pathways are often evidenced by hirsutism and amenorrhea in women. (These signs can be grossly augmented with prolonged administration of the phenothiazines.) Furthermore, there is recent evidence that endorphin metabolism is abnormal in schizophrenic psychosis. These metabolic problems will concern us again in Chapter 8.

Schizophrenic people often seem to have clinical or subclinical cardiovascular and nutritional disorders as well. Even when such pictures cannot be demonstrated, many schizophrenic patients present a vague appearance of physiological and metabolic dysfunction. The hair is lacking in luster and order. The skin is sallow, dry or waxy. The face is flaccid or overly taut, and the body is overly thin or else flaccidly obese. As the relatives say, the patient just doesn't look good. But we must bear in mind that these dysfunctions can be attributed to the core-brain disturbances which I shall describe later.

There is another dimension of general appearance which is worthy of mention. We are a people who constantly rate ourselves and others on the basis of contemporary standards of attractiveness. On this basis the majority of schizophrenic people strike us as attractive. They do not seem to be interesting, likable or sexy, for instance. But true to the schizophrenic proclivity to extremes, there are striking exceptions. Some schizophrenic patients appear especially winsome or intriguing, and some show a heightening of sexuality and an appearance of extraordinary beauty. A number of people who won fame in the arts or in the theater on the basis of such positively valued traits were schizophrenic people who later became psychotic hospital patients.

There is one other dimension of organismic "health" which intrigued many investigators in past decades. There are vastly different tissue reactions and morbidity rates in the various subtypes of schizophrenia. Lewis (1936) showed many decades ago that paranoid hospital patients show hyperplastic tissue reactions at autopsy. Such reactions are characterized by organ enlargements, tissue overgrowth, excessive scarring and so on. The hebephrenic and catatonic patients examined by Lewis showed hypoplasia and hypodevelopment of tissues and organs. A generation ago I demonstrated that paranoid patients have higher cancer rates than the general population, while in catatonic and hebephrenic patients the cancer rates are much lower than those of the general population. Furthermore, paranoid patients get malignancies at an earlier age than the general population and show a more rapid progression and a greater degree of malignancy. We are tempted to postulate a correlation between the overactivity of paranoid people and an overproliferation of tissue and cellular growth.

Biologically and medically oriented investigators have traditionally tended to ascribe these deviations in health and nutrition to schizophrenia itself. Said otherwise, these deviations in organismic states have been classed with the behavioral and cognitive disorders as symptoms of the underlying schizophrenic disease. But we must bear in mind two contradictory observations. First of all, none of these deviations is characteristic of the classic schizophrenic. They occur in only some instances of schizophrenia. In the second place, disorders of health and nutrition can and do reflect peculiarities in the lifestyles of psychotic people. Some schizophrenic people live year after year in a state of impassivity, while others live in a continuous state of rage. Some psychotic people do not eat adequately, or they eat only carrots or raw meat. Many never go outdoors or expose themselves to the sunshine, and this avoidance is heightened if they are taking thorazine.

In short, one can argue that deviations in our usual indices of health and nutrition accrue from living in a continuing psychotic state. Most contemporary students of schizophrenia incline to this view, though the orthomolecular psychiatrists constitute a notable exception. In this approach, schizophrenia is said to be a B-vitamin deficiency on the basis of some similarities between schizophrenic psychosis and the psychosis of pellagra (Pauling, 1968).*

Bodily Tonus and Activity Levels

In my experience, all schizophrenic people show a deviation in level of activity and in bodily tonus—either a marked elevation or a marked reduction. Those with acute psychotic disorganizations and paranoid trends are endlessly overactive. They flee and pace. They move from location to location or, when they are obliged to remain in a space or a room, from posture to posture. At the very least they show a fidgeting restlessness of the hands and feet and a constantly shifting gaze. In these tense and active patients there is usually an extremely high state of muscular tonus. Sometimes there is also a general rigidity, though this is not usually a rigidity of the cogwheel type as is seen in Parkinsonian states. This rigidity is currently attributed to the phenothiazines, but it was observed before these drugs began to be employed, and it is now sometimes observable in schizophrenic patients who have not yet been administered these medications.

In contrast to the schizophrenic type described above, many "schizoid" or pre-psychotic people are markedly underactive. They

---

* Personally, I am not impressed with this rationale. The neurological picture of thiamine deficiency is quite clear-cut and not like that of schizophrenia. The dementia of pellagra is also not very like the psychosis of schizophrenia, and there is no evidence that scurvy and other vitamin deficiencies are characteristic in schizophrenia. The fact that some psychotic people improve on an orthomolecular regime does not support the rationale either. Many psychotic patients will show a temporary improvement whenever they receive a new medication, a reason to believe in it, a regime of activity and an increased measure of optimistic support from staff and relatives.

I am not on these accounts opposed to an orthomolecular regime. That the regime does not support its rationale does not mean that it is not beneficial to the patient. This topic is discussed in detail by Crider (1979).

stay home day after day or sit for hours without changing locations. They resist any attempts to get them involved in work, play or conversation. They do not even shift posture very often, and sometimes they are motionless except for an oscillatory swinging of one leg or an occasional grimace or smile. This sort of marked inactivity is also seen in chronically psychotic patients. With these states of inactivity there is usually a marked reduction in bodily tonus. The face sags, the shoulders slouch, and the abdominal wall is flabby. We can see that the paranoid experiences a hypertonicity, while the bemused and resigned hebephrenic is inert and flaccid.

The deviation in tonus and activity in schizophrenia is accompanied by a very high or a very low level of alertness or attentiveness. The chronically psychotic patient is sometimes almost impervious to outside noises or the actions of other people, while the acutely psychotic or paranoid patient is extremely distractible.

A host of psychological procedures demonstrate increase or decrease in attentiveness in schizophrenia. We can also spot a low or high degree of attention in the clinical situation. The patient with low attentiveness drifts into fantasy and fails to hear what is said to him. In the middle of a conversation his eyes and head drop, his body becomes flaccid, and he gives the appearance of falling into reverie and detachment. Conversely, the schizophrenic patient with high arousal or distractibility sits in a high degree of tonus, moves about almost incessantly, shifts gaze very frequently and turns to attend the slightest noise from an adjoining room.

Clinicians sometimes speak of the level of consciousness when they are referring to arousal or attentiveness. In my view this is too narrow a usage for the concept of consciousness. This issue will concern us later in this chapter and again in Chapter 6.

Bodily tonus is also related in a specific way to the degree of sexuality or the readiness for courtship. In an actual courtship, for instance, both parties show a marked increase of bodily tonus and alertion. The facial and abdominal muscles are tautly drawn so that sags and bulges tend to disappear. The arm and leg muscles become apparent, giving the sexy look which is imitated so well by actresses and models. By contrast, those who are disinterested in sexual thoughts and contacts tend to show a low tonus. The lids, chin and abdominal muscles sag.

The belly protrudes. The torso and arms appear flaccid, and the face is placid or flaccid.

In pre-psychotic schizophrenia and in chronically psychotic instances, this low tonus appears and is accompanied by a low interest in sexuality. But occasionally the opposite picture appears, as usual in its extreme form. Such high states of courtship readiness may be accompanied by sexual promiscuity or an immense sexual preoccupation; in the case of women, this appearance can lead to rape or sexual exploitation. Some paranoid patients evidence an intermediate courtship tonus, which is perceived as a high degree of charisma. In any event, deviation in either direction of bodily tonus, alertness and sexual readiness is characteristic of schizophrenia.

Needs, Drives and Vegetative States

The degree of sexual readiness or libido is also one aspect of another dimension of bodily states and of motor activity (see Chapter 6). In neurology, these are sometimes called vegetative functions, but in the psychological sciences they are more likely to be attributed to instincts, drives or needs. In addition to sexual arousal they include levels of appetite and the readiness to fight or flee.*

There is one other aspect of involuntary bodily activity which is commonly dysfunctional in schizophrenia. The patient shows an overactivity of either the sympathetic or parasympathetic system and is thus judged to have an autonomic imbalance. In the 1930s a vast literature accumulated on autonomic activity in psychosis, and an imbalance in autonomic function was sometimes considered to play a causal role in schizophrenia. Nowadays we do not hold this view. We simply regard the autonomic disturbances as part of the general emotional upheaval and nueral disorganization of psychosis.

In any event, the schizophrenic patient is likely to show a dilated or a constricted pupil, an excess in skin pallor, sweating or excessive skin dryness, an elevated or slowed pulse rate, excessive or reduced bowel and bladder mobility, and other autonomic dysfunctions.

---

* Pribram (1971) speaks of these functions as the four "f's": fighting, flight, feeding and fucking.

These are not, however, considered as specific to or diagnostic of the schizophrenic condition.

These vegetative functions are characteristically heightened or diminished in schizophrenia. In schizoid types or pre-psychotic people, a lack of hunger and a low level of sexuality or courtship readiness are often marked, while in some states of psychosis there is an insatiable need for food and sometimes a marked sexual preoccupation. In many pre-psychotic and chronically psychotic people, there is also a very low level of belligerence and a constant readiness for flight, while in some paranoid patients a readiness to fight is an outstanding feature.

Mood in Schizophrenia

An important aspect of physiological states in schizophrenia is a deviation in mood. In most non-psychotic and borderline patients, as well as in psychotic states, there is an overriding mood of ahedonia, dysphoria or sadness which may deepen to an overt depression at certain times, such as the period when an acute psychosis is abating. Less often the psychotic patient experiences periods of euphoria or even hypomania. When these affective features are prominent in the psychosis, together with clearly schizophrenic signs, the diagnosis of schizoaffective schizophrenia is made. As I said in Chapter 1, such variants of the schizophrenic psychosis are more common in people of Mediterranean or African origin (not necessarily in American black people). If marked manic or cyclic reactions occur without schizophrenic disturbances in cognition and motor behavior, the diagnosis of "manic-depressive" psychosis is made. But depression and hypomanic states are less common in schizophrenia in this country than are gross disturbances in other moods. High levels of anxiety or even panic occur episodically in non-psychotic schizophrenic people, and these often characterize the psychotic episodes of schizophrenia.

EMOTIONALITY IN SCHIZOPHRENIA

Clinicians combine their observations of many of these bodily or physiological states and designate them as disorders of emotion. Let us ask first what dimensions of bodily behavior are so embraced. They include levels of activity and bodily tonus, degree of arousal, attentiveness and distractibility, the vegetative functions of sexuality, appetite and the readiness to fight or flee, signs of autonomic activity and mood. There are two other dimensions of mood which we have not yet discussed. The patient may report a disorder of mood by means of speech or show obvious bodily and facial sets that indicate panic, depression, hostility or euphoria. Also, an inability to complete a linear task or a narrative is taken as evidence of emotional disturbance (see Chapter 6).

If we consider these indicators of emotion collectively, we can generalize that schizophrenia is characterized by an emotional disturbance in either direction from our cultural norms. The level of emotionality is either heightened or diminished. In pre-psychotic conditions and in chronic states of schizophrenic psychosis, the emotional indicators are diminished, and the patient is said to show a flattening of affect. In acute psychosis, in the schizoaffective types and sometimes in paranoid psychoses, the indicators of emotionality are increased. The patient could be said to have a "fattened" affectivity.

But whatever the direction of emotional deviance, *some deviance is characteristic of schizophrenic and psychotic states.* Said otherwise, an emotional disturbance characterizes schizophrenia and its psychoses. Since the deviation can be in either direction, we can say that the schizophrenic person suffers a relative inability to sustain emotional modulation.

If we are very careful about how we interpret our generalization, we can say that this inability to modulate arousal, extrapyramidal functions, mood, and vegetative functions is mediated in the corebrain. But here is where we must exercise care. That emotional states are mediated in the corebrain *does not necessarily indicate that a corebrain lesion is present in schizophrenia, nor that these disturbances originate in the corebrain.* The fact is that visceral afferents and limbic pathways normally exercise a cybernetic control or regulatory function upon the corebrain and neuraxis and thus place them under the influence of physiological states and of the cerebral cortex.

We can now make our first guess about the bodily physiological dysfunctions in schizophrenia. We can surmise that they reflect some imbalance or loss of integration within the larger organization of the central nervous system. We can also surmise that secondary physiological dysfunctions can accrue from sustained corebrain dysfunction and the peculiar life-styles and habits of some psychotic people. We will add another dimension of this view in Chapter 6 when we discuss psychological processes and neural organization as a whole.

ON DEGREES OF PSYCHOSIS

Kraepelin (1906) originally held that there were four types of schizophrenia—the simple, the paranoid, the hebephrenic and the catatonic. Later on he changed his classification, and Bleuler employed another one (1950). Since then various theorists and committes have revised these classifications again and again. These revisions have apparently been carried out with one eye on the politics of expediency and discipline, and the other on the belief that there are such things as absolute categories.

General Problems of Diagnosis

If you have ever tried to classify the books in your library by topics, you are well aware of the impossibilities of an absolute classification. Some books fit into several of your categories, and some do not fit any of them. The myth is that you can solve this problem by tinkering with the categories. If you try to do so, you will eventually be exhausted by the effort. But you will be even more confused if your classification is also transsected by other considerations. Suppose, for example, that you also want to have some books closer to your desk for ready reference or suppose that you wish to display some of them more prominently to impress visitors with your erudition or your main systems of belief.

These very problems have plagued the periodic attempts of the American Psychiatric Association to reclassify mental "illnesses." For example, it was not possible to clearly locate all cases of schizophrenia in the Kraepelinian categories that were employed in *DSM-I*. No one wanted to bother with them either, so a class of "undifferentiated schizophrenia" was introduced. After this, almost all clinicians found it simpler to use this class, and other types of schizophrenics seemed to virtually disappear from our statistical reviews.

To make matters more bewitching, certain members of these committees have been cognizant of conceptual fads. In *DSM-II*, for instance, it was deemed wise to call schizophrenia a reaction, for that era recognized a social aspect to the schizophrenic problem.

These Talmudic machinations do have an important value. Concepts like "diagnosis," "chronic" and "type" do support the sacredness of the medical model of disease and its psychological equivalent. Also, they do keep the power of diagnosis in the hands of the medical profession, since most governments and institutions require that a physician confirm the diagnosis in accordance with the Diagnostic and Statistical Manual of the American Psychiatric Association (or the institution will not get its fiscal allotment). But all this hullabaloo does nothing for the patient and nothing towards the understanding of deviation and schizophrenia. In fact, one can argue that medical terms and concepts like "process" schizophrenia are injurious to the patient, for they imply a poor prognosis, and they place the blame for that poor prognosis upon the characteristics of the schizophrenic condition. Thus, they obscure the fact that the prognosis may depend upon adverse institutional practices and inadequate or adversive treatments.

For these reasons, many of us quarrel with the implications and politics of the whole ritual of diagnosis. But we quarrel in vain. The diagnostics and the subtyping of schizophrenia are an ongoing process, and I cannot refuse to deal with it in a book on schizophrenia. In the following pages, I will cover the issue of schizophrenic subtypes, by first declaring my own views or biases on the subject, and then arguing that the problem of subtypes has not yet been placed in a useful perspective.

My own views include the following. First of all, I think the classical subtypes of schizophrenia refer to the *psychotic states* of schizophrenia, for we have not yet achieved even a tentative classification of non-psychotic schizophrenia. Secondly, in spite of my anti-Kraepelinian positions, I think that Kraepelin's original list of simple, paranoid, hebephrenic and catatonic fits the clinical phenomena of schizophrenia far better than any classifications which have been perpetuated since Kraepelin. Thirdly, I think we must either forget classifications or use those which have some clarity and strength of category. A classification which allows noncategories such as mixed, undifferentiated or "other" is absurd. Can we imagine a classification of seasons which included "winter," "spring," "summer," "fall," "undifferentiated," and "other"?

I think that the designation of a schizoaffective category is not so easy to dismiss. Yet a preponderance of mood disturbances does not change the criteria for designating the critical differences in cognition or neural organization. In psychosis, all corebrain activities and organismic states are disturbed. We do not make a separate category of "anxiety schizophrenia" for those who show an especially marked degree of panic.*

On these grounds we cannot be so sure that various types of patients characteristically develop a given type of psychosis. Instead we must entertain the possibility that there are degrees of psychotic disorganization. I hesitate to use the term "stages" because I do not want to buy into the Kraepelinian notion of a progressive and irreversible deterioration. The fact is that in America the type of psychosis is not seen as an index of prognosis, and we can observe that a patient who is in a catatonic stupor one day may show simple cognitive disorganization a week later. This was the case long before phenothiazines were introduced.

If we judge these degrees of psychosis on the basis of upheaval in bodily states and the loss of order in motor behavior, we can propose a series of greater severity. In Kraepelinian terms, this would begin with the simple type as least disorganized; then we would regard as more disorganized the paranoid, then the hebephrenic, and then the catatonic types. But I think we can differentiate these degrees of psychosis more clearly if we use somewhat different terms and criteria than those of the classical Kraepelinian subtypes.

I shall tackle the important issue of psychotic subtypes by introducing it with a brief characterization of four degrees of schizo-

---

* In Part I, I said that the schizoaffective types were more often from non-Northern cultures. It seems also probable that such people suffer the social and molecular problems of both schizophrenia and the depressive series of psychosis.

phrenic psychosis which resemble Kraepelin's subtypes. Then, in Chapter 7, I will describe the basis for these differentiations of degree in terms of progressive disorganizations in the relations of neural subsystems in the cerebrum and the brain stem. This effort will allow us to make some explanations of the differences in clinical picture and the contexts of their occurrence.

Before I begin, I would like to explain an important difference between the concept of degrees and the more classical view of types in a classification. If a schizophrenic person shows a shift in psychosis from degree one to degree two, the *behaviors of the first degree of psychosis do not necessarily disappear*. Thus, advances in the degree of psychosis show an *accumulation* of psychotic dysfunctions. The patient does not simply shift from one kind of psychosis to another.

The Problem of Accumulated Dysfunctions

Certain schizophrenic patients develop the same kind of psychotic picture *every time they have a psychotic episode*. In addition, they remain paranoid or hebephrenic or catatonic as long as that psychotic episode persists—sometimes for years. We can further sometimes discover that the psychotic type in these patients was heralded by suspiciousness, silliness or stubbornness even in childhood.

This sort of patient gives strength to the notion that there are quite different types of schizophrenia. In fact, we could argue that paranoid psychotics must be different from catatonic ones on the basis of genetics, early experience and personality. But there is more to the problem. Many schizophrenic people are hebephrenic one day and paranoid the next. Some even change from one subtype to another from hour to hour or in the course of an interview. When we try to put together the differences between our observations and the nurse's notes, we fall back in confusion on the diagnosis of "undifferentiated type." We can also observe that some schizophrenic people move from a simple to a paranoid to a catatonic type of picture in a sequence of days or weeks, so we are inclined to view them as passing through states in a progressive deterioration.

We can sometimes notice as well that the type of psychosis is related to the manner in which the patient is handled. Many a quietly disorganized patient becomes paranoid when he is interviewed by a disdainful, tired and hostile examiner. Sometimes a hebephrenic patient becomes catatonic when he is strong-armed by a zealous staff.

The First State of Psychosis

The schizophrenic person goes along day by day making an adjustment of sorts; then a psychotic episode occurs—sometimes without evident reason. It may develop in a matter of hours or escalate slowly over a period of days or weeks. The barometer is anxiety. It begins with a vague uneasy feeling and increases to a terrifying panic, especially in those who have never been markedly psychotic before.

In this first stage of disorganization, there is a characteristic change in observable behavior. The increasingly psychotic person cannot perform even simple operations. There is an inability to remember what sequence is to be followed in a task. The goal or image, even the next step, is lost from consciousness.

The psychotic person will tell us about this. There seems to be a distractibility, an inability to remember even the most familiar steps. Other subjective phenomena occur too. One of the most common of these is the loss of the sense of spatial order, a loss of form and boundary. A loss of the sense of identity also occurs. The psychotic is not sure who he is. He feels strange, alienated from others and unfamiliar. Sometimes the psychotic is not certain he is not his mother or father or someone else; there can be a sense of physical fusion with another. In psychoanalytic terms, there is a loss of ego boundaries. With these strange experiences, anxiety mounts to panic. There is marked hypertonus, loss of appetite, even a flight reaction.

Second Stage of Psychosis

The psychotic disorganization may proceed no further than this first stage, perhaps because these frightening and strange manifestations bring control and assistance. Often, however, the disorganization proceeds to a second stage, in which the behavior and experiences of the first stage may be continued but a new set of phenomena is added. These consist of striking perceptual changes. Familiar things and people look different, and the changes are interpreted as mystical and dangerous. Sensory images are projected to sensory organs or even to spaces outside the body. Thoughts, for example, are experienced as voices. These are the hallucinatory phenomena of the psychosis. They may be of an auditory, visual, sensory, olfactory and/or gustatory nature.

With these occurrences the psychotic person may become belligerent. The marked degree of bodily tension and arousal already evident may even increase. There is marked or extreme hyperactivity. In addition to a fight reaction, there are marked disturbances in other vegetative functions. This stage of psychotic disorganization is ordinarily termed a paranoid psychosis. It may have precursors for many years, or this paranoid reaction may occur as a second stage of disorganization following the loss of sequence, spatial order and identity. It may occur instead of the first stage or along with it, so that both pictures develop together. Then we speak of an "acute undifferentiated psychosis."

A Third Degree of Disorganization

There may be a further disorganization in behavior, thought and emotional modulation. Total distractibility and inattentiveness may appear. The psychotic becomes unable to speak coherently or to think except in a totally confused and fragmentary way. The hallucinatory phenomena continue. Sleep, eating and sexuality are impossible or, sometimes, grossly fluctuating. Depression or hypomania may be added to anxiety and anger. In this form of psychosis, complete alienation and withdrawal are likely to occur and, with them, the hypotonic, inert behaviors of "chronic" schizophrenia. The patient may stand in one spot all day, for instance, or sit hunched over and almost motionless in a corner of the ward.

Fourth Stage of Psychosis

In the deepest form of disorientation, the inability to organize any behavior continues, along with the perceptual disorders of stage two. The body may now be slumped in an almost fetal position with little activity except for manneristic movements. There is a complete disorientation of time and place and a marked memory loss. The patient seems to be in a trance or dreamlike state; the term "nightmare" might be more appropriate. With this state there is often an incessant oscillatory or rocking movement of the body, usually in children, or, in adults, a rhythmical movement of some part of the body. Sometimes this is a head nodding; most often the patient crosses his legs and moves the upper leg in an endless oscillatory upward and downward arc. Sometimes the eyes move from side to side. Modern clinicians often attribute these oscillatory movements to antipsychotic medication. I do not doubt that drugs enhance them, but we saw these movements in our hospitals long before antipsychotic drugs were discovered.

DEFINING THE CLASS OF ALL SCHIZOPHRENICS

Before we go on to describe in Chapter 6 the motor behavior of schizophrenia, we must try to agree about what behavior is schizophrenic, i.e., what behavior is found in all of the people we label schizophrenic. If we are to move forward in this effort, we have to have some ground rules. First, we must limit our contributions to statements about behavior. We should agree to describe patterns of behavior and withhold our theories about cause and our inferences about emotion, thought or motive for another occasion. Second, we must have some agreement about what reason or logic to use. Suppose we use the very logic we say the schizophrenics cannot use, the Aristotelian approach of defining a class and the members of that class. Or we can use one of the more modern versions of this logic, such as the proposition of sets. Let us, however, use the broader American view of the term schizophrenia and include the subset of schizophrenic people who are not psychotic.

Since we are to define the behaviors of all schizophrenic people, we can start by excluding those behaviors which are enacted only by some schizophrenic people or which show only on certain occasions, such as during a psychotic episode. But I must be more specific; I must name some of these behaviors. Some of the people we call schizophrenic never show the behaviors to be described in Chapter 6, and many do not show them all of the time. Many schizophrenic people do not speak or act as if they are seeing visions or hearing voices, and they do not act as if they are being followed or persecuted. In other words, all schizophrenic people (by American standards) do not show Schneider's "first-rank symptoms" of visible or audible projection. In addition, all schizophrenic people do not show silly, histrionic behavior. They do not necessarily tell us that they do not know who they are or what date it is, and they do not seem visibly perplexed or confused. All schizophrenic people do not regularly lie or sit in a stupor or race about in a wild state of excitement. Relatively few act as if they are continuously experiencing a dream or nightmare.

The schizophrenic people who do act like this are said (in America) to be psychotic. But we do not on this account say or imply that they are no longer schizophrenic. The fact is that schizophrenics who are psychotic are also schizophrenic, and the class of psychotic schizophrenics is a subclass of schizophrenia in time and type. If we want to be fancy, we can draw a Venn diagram to show our conclusion:

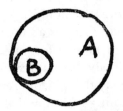

Where the circle (A) includes
all people we call schizophrenic,
and subscribe (B) includes those
who are *also* psychotic.

One final point is that we must remember the relativity of our judgment on this. Since schizophrenia is a Western, industrial concept, we must only include those people who have been exposed to its educational and social modes without being able to accomplish them.

6

The Behavior of

Schizophrenia

I have moved blithely through Chapter 5 without acknowledging a glaring omission. I have described the organismic behavior of schizophrenia without mentioning either speech or other forms of motor behavior. Certainly we cannot paint a picture of the total person without saying what he says and does; also, there are serious disorders of neuromuscular behavior in schizophrenia.

The behavior of schizophrenic people is deviant from our usual social norms, and by most standards it is maladaptive. We can conceive of two aspects of this deviation. In one, we observe that the behavior is inappropriate to its context, and we have traditionally dealt with this aspect by abstracting the deviance. Concepts such as "autistic" or "overdependent" are examples. The second sort of deviance is a disorder of form or patterning. For instance, the schizophrenic tells a story or works at a physical task but gets the steps out of order. Both approaches to schizophrenic behavior will be described here.

Although these descriptions will remedy the omission of behavior and allow us to complete our picture of the organismic level, they will bring us to two other theoretical problems. If I do not anticipate these now, I may alienate both the systems theorists and the psychologically-oriented reader. The system theorist will ask on what grounds I consider motor behavior a level of organization and why I insert it at this point in a schema of levels. And those of a psychological orientation may bristle because I do not deal with cognition or ego functioning in this chapter. I will deal with the problem of levels later in this chapter, and I will cover psychological abstractions in Chapter 7, for although these are made by observing motor behavior, they refer to the organization of cortical and corebrain processes. For the present, then, I will get on with a description of motor behavior, including speech.

SOME ABSTRACTIONS ABOUT SCHIZOPHRENIC BEHAVIOR

In the early part of the twentieth century a dichotomy evolved between two views of behavior. In one, common in academic psychology, behavior was seen as a response to stimuli. In the other, common in psychodynamic approaches, behavior was seen as an expression of thoughts, emotions, or needs. Since a great deal of our literature about the behavior of schizophrenia used to be divided on this basis, I will briefly characterize some examples of each category. Fortunately, our contemporary literature on schizophrenia acknowledges both views, and nowadays it is difficult to understand why the proponents of these two doctrinal approaches took so many decades to realize that the nervous system (and the person) responds to sensory inputs *and* initiates its own patterns of action.

Schizophrenic Adjustment

Descriptive terms such as "withdrawn," "defensive" or "paranoid" reflect the schizophrenic problems of social adjustment. Other terms like "overdependent" or "orally regressed" attend to another aspect of schizophrenic relationships. These psychoanalytic terms refer to personality abstractions about behavior. In Chapter 7, I will review some psychoanalytic views of intrapsychic or ego processes in schizophrenia. These two aspects of schizophrenic behavior—social adjustment and intrapsychic functioning—are spelled out more carefully in personality appraisals of characteristic and persistent schizophrenic reactions. Two such appraisals are usually made about schizophrenic people and are often criteria for the diagnosis. Since I have discussed these in some detail in Part I, I will only characterize them here.

1) *Schizophrenic people are distant, defensive or withdrawn in their behavior to most of the people around them.* In extreme cases there is an avoidance of all social participation; less extremely, the behavior of social contact is fleeting, engagement is formal, polite, constrained and temporary. A few schizophrenic people employ charisma, sexuality, amiability and other winsome approaches to form fleeting contact with other people. Rarely, such behavior is employed to attract and exploit followers and cult members, but on the whole schizophrenic people avoid intimate, mutual and prolonged relationships with most (but not all) other people.

2) *In spite of this general pattern of distance and avoidance, schizophrenic people are usually attached in a markedly dependent way to one partner or family member and occasionally to the family as a whole or to some institution.* However, this dependent attachment varies markedly in its characteristics and overtness. At one extreme there is a childlike dependency on the "symbiotic partner" (Mahler and La Perriere 1965), in which the schizophrenic person takes little initiative without approval or instructions from the partner. Dependency can be concealed with a display of independence, an obstinate disobedience or an avoidance of the partner; yet the dependency is evidenced in the consistent inability of the schizophrenic person to initiate alternative relationships, independent plans or a self-sustaining life-style. Together these reactions appear as a marked ambivalence toward the partner. This ambivalence was a criterion for the diagnosis of schizophrenia in Bleuler's original description of the primary behaviors of schizophrenia (Bleuler, 1950).

Collectively, this difficulty in relating to people and institutional standards and the overt or concealed dependence results in a failure to meet conventional social standards and a life pattern of social and institutional failures. A vicious cycle of social failure and a fear of closeness and dependency can evolve.

In part, the withdrawal of schizophrenic people can be interpreted as a fear of being dependent. In such a view the independence can be seen as evidence of overly dependent needs. In any event, the fearful avoidance of closeness and the failure to develop autonomous activities give evidence of a proclivity for depending heavily on a partner.

The schizophrenic's overattachment to an original partner and fear of forming new attachments can make it hard to form a therapeutic alliance with him. Many therapists who say that it is impossible to form contact with schizophrenic patients make an effort to do so, but do not seem to know how. Some therapists, however, are remarkably able to develop relationships with schizophrenic people. John Rosen could do so quickly with even the most paranoid patient (Rosen, 1953; Scheflen, 1960a). In my view he did so with a combination of aggressive insistence and continuous reassurance that the patient would be released from custody and control as soon as he was able to take care of himself (Scheflen, 1960a).

Another common personality pattern I have observed in schizophrenic patients has received little attention. Most are very rigid and resistant to change. Not only do schizophrenic people resist changing their own behavior, but they also resist any changes in their partners and their few relationships. They fear a display of emotions from those they depend upon. They fear desertion, and they resent even a shift in furniture, decor or housing conditions. In my view, this rigidity stems from a need for constancy in a field of cues to prevent a psychotic disorganization.

A triad of social avoidance, overdependency and rigidity often characterizes the behavioral repertoire of schizophrenics. But there is another level to this set of characteristics that we must not forget. The overdependency, the fear of new relationships and a serious rigidity in life-style are often shared by the partner of the schizophrenic or even by the family as a whole. In this case, these traits are part of a social contract or an unwitting conspiracy. These points are illustrated by an especially interesting patient whom I shall call Robert.

After a psychotic break, it was decided that Robert must move out of his parental household and have his own apartment. This was painfully accomplished, and Robert lived alone every day and evening. But at eleven o'clock every night—as soon as his parents had gone to bed—Robert would return to his parents' apartment and to his previous bedroom. Here his mother had carefully preserved all of his childhood toys, including a favorite teddy bear, and all of his school memorabilia. She also left the key for him so he could enter the house. Robert would play with these objects all night, leaving the parental household early the next morning before his parents awakened. On two occasions he was stopped from doing this—once by his father and once by a therapist who was pushing "psychosexual maturation." On both occasions Robert became grossly psychotic again. From then on everyone quietly acquiesced to this interesting Proserpine-like arrangement.

There are other dimensions of adjustment that are not characteristic of schizophrenic people as a group. A few attain extraordinary creativity, especially in the arts. Some schizophrenic people are quite warm, while others are icy cold (English, 1962). Despite many life failures, some schizophrenic people, preoccupied with power and dominance, are designing, tricky, overbearing and belittling. Others accept a passive subservient role and present an obsequious manner. A tall handsome schizophrenic patient once told me, "I am a rabbit. I stay in my hole because everytime I stick my head out, the world has a big role for me to play." Some schizophrenic people play the scapegoat or the fool; others insidiously construct double-binds and make all life efforts seem absurd. Still others live a life of passive obedience, even while they defeat all of our therapeutic efforts.

Fantasy and the Preoccupations of Schizophrenics

Freud defined a psychodynamic view as a view of behavioral patterns of response to life situations and to the accrual of childhood experience. In recent decades, simplistic depreciations of this view have led many clinicians to view behavior as mere expression of thoughts and emotions. In such a model, the behavior of schizophrenic people is attributed to their mentalistic preoccupations, and schizophrenic people are brought into psychotherapy and encouraged to talk about what is on their minds. Accordingly, there is a huge literature on the memories, thoughts and fantasies of schizophrenic people.

If you ask what schizophrenic people talk about, the simplest answer is "anything under the sun." Personally, I have had schizophrenic patients who would talk for months, if I did not intervene, about such subjects as the following: how to become the fourth Musketeer; how it might feel to suck the marrow out of father's femur; the possibilities of sexual intercourse with grandmother; or a plan to set fire to the firehouse. In spite of many reports about the imaginative and rich fantasy life of schizophrenic patients, in my experience most such patients have a few stereotyped subjects. They will talk about these forever with the naive therapist who will listen patiently and voyeuristically without demanding any change in the patient's thoughts or activities.

There also seem to be some themes of thought and preoccupations which are characteristic of schizophrenics. The first of these is a preoccupation with self-evaluations, including past failures, reviews of self and bodily image, and dreams of imaginary or wished-for accomplishments. The second subject is criticism of the possessiveness, untrustworthiness, greed, controlling tactics and shortcomings of other people in general or of the symbiotic partner in particular.

Nevertheless, I suspect that the ideation which is elicited from any patient depends in part on the interests of the therapist, so other clinicians may have very different impressions of the preoccupations of schizophrenic patients. Furthermore, most clinical papers dwell upon *interpretations* of what the patient says in therapy rather that with what is said.

Another question about the thoughts of schizophrenic people warrants our attention. We should ask what paradigms or explanatory principles schizophrenic people tend to use to account for their experiences. In general, of course, they use the same paradigms as any other member of the society, i.e., biological, psychological or social explanations. But the schizophrenic is often very conservative in his epistemology. He thinks like a classical Aristotelian, believing that some concrete entity, some person or thing, is the cause of it all, and imagining unseen forces that govern his experience. In the paranoid instance, he "discovers" who his enemy is, and he comes to "know" just what forces or influences are being used against him.

The Emergence of More Combined Views

Contemporary clinicians tend to employ integrative views of schizophrenic adjustment and expression. Searles has written much about the phenomenology of schizophrenic thought from a psychoanalytic viewpoint, but he has also published a classical paper on dependency in schizophrenia (1955). Mahler (1963) and her associates (Mahler and La Perriere, 1965) have observed mother-infant relationships in childhood psychosis and have made psychoanalytic formulations of early schizophrenia. Arieti (1955, 1974), also a psychoanalyst, has written prolifically on both the psychoanalytic and the social aspects of schizophrenic behavior.

PSYCHOLOGICAL TESTS AND EXPERIMENTS

There is a voluminous literature on testing and psychological experiments with schizophrenic subjects. Certain problems plague these psychological approaches to the understanding of schizophrenia, however. First, most papers keep measuring the same variables and reaffirming generalizations which everyone already accepts. Secondly, there are traditional lines of research in which paper after paper repeats the same general approach with some variations in procedure, but each challenges the reliability and validity of the others so the final result is an uncertainty in both findings and interpretations.* In all fairness to psychology, one must point out that clinical observations and biological studies suffer the very same problems. This will become clearer in Part III. Here I will mention a few psychological test and experimental findings from studies which were carried out in the psychological paradigm. In Chapter 7, I will review a large number of psychological approaches in the newer neurophysiological tradition.

A variety of projective techniques have been used in the diagnosis and study of schizophrenia. Of these the best known and most carefully studied is the Rorschach. Like other projectives, these tests

---

* I am forever intrigued by the way experimentalists and clinicians alike confuse behavioral observations and heuristic inferences. They observe verbal or paper-and-pencil responses or they watch sorting behavior or some other motor activity, but they say they have thereby studied thought, cognition or ego processes.

show that schizophrenic subjects tend to use unusual interpretations of form and explicate them rather poorly. For example, there are high minus scores for form (F minus), for originality (O minus), and movement (M minus). In addition, the Rorschach commonly shows that schizophrenic people select a part of the total card as a focus of observation and elaborate this part as if it were the whole stimulus. There is also Rorschach evidence of a problem in overconcreteness or overabstraction; this finding accords with the traditional line of research I will describe next.

Over 40 years ago Kurt Goldstein claimed certain similarities between schizophrenic and brain-damaged patients on the basis that both groups tend to be overly literal or concrete, or else overly abstract or metaphorical. On this basis, he and his colleagues (Goldstein, 1951) developed sorting tasks to test the deviations. So did Vigotsky (cited by Goldstein, 1951). Since then, a variety of these tests have been used. This tradition of study is still being employed and has been reported recently by Harrow et al. (1972). These tests show deviations such as the linking of unrelated items (Goldstein, 1951), or an overinclusion of items in a particular category (Harrow et al., 1972). Von Domarus (1951) interpreted these findings as pointing to a disorder in which items with one common aspect were conceived as being identical. Angyal (1951) claimed that schizophrenic pepole misidentified the characteristics of a class or set. It should be noted that these interpretations are comparable to what Bateson et al. (1956) described as a problem in logical types or a problem in the relation of item and class. (These findings will concern us again in Chapter 7.)

There is another line of experimental study and measurement that has been developed largely by Chapman and Chapman (1973) and by Shakow (1962). This approach measures the distractibility or attentiveness of schizophrenic people and finds, of course, an impairment. But the way these tests are conducted provides less obvious and more interesting findings. Subjects are asked, for instance, to respond to multiple choices about the meaning of certain words. The results show problems of understanding sets, somewhat as I have already described. From these and other such experiences, Shakow (1962) has evolved a segmental-set hypothesis of schizophrenia.

Simply stated, Shakow postulates major and minor sets and postulates that schizophrenic people confuse these and thus suffer the distraction of an attention to one set when they are supposedly operating in another. Here again, let us postpone further consideration of these views until Chapter 7 in the discussion of cognition and cerebral integration.

DEVIATIONS IN THE STRUCTURE OF BEHAVIOR

In the psychological sciences, we characteristically observe a stream of behavior and then make abstractions of its qualities, or we make psychodynamic interpretations of the motives of the behavior. But in some sciences the primary attention of study is directed at the form or pattern of the activity. A classical example is structural linguistics, in which the sequencing of sounds and syntax of speech are the object of research. In the systems era, a number of other sciences have evolved which attend closely to the structure of behavior, for example, ethology and the "structural" approaches to communication. The observations I have already made on the behaviors of interaction derive from this approach. So does the "double-bind theory" (Bateson et al., 1956) of schizophrenia, which is in part based on observing conflicting messages in the behavior of schizophrenic family members. We should ask what else the "structuralist" has to say about the behavioral patterns in schizophrenia.

Speech and the Clinical Concept of a Thought Disorder

The descriptive psychiatrists of past generations listened to chronically psychotic hospital patients and made descriptions of various disorders in speech. They described the neologisms (or newly composed words), word-salads and clang associations (the association of words that rhyme). Speech was often described as totally rambling and illogical. Nowadays we do not so often observe these gross disorders of the structure of speech, and we attribute them to chronic psychosis rather than considering them to be characteristic of schizophrenia as a whole.

Clinicians still listen to the speech of schizophrenic people, but they are more likely to use its form and content to make inferences about schizophrenic thought. In the milder degrees of psychosis, it is often noticed that the trend of thought is interrupted with distractions. Thoughts are not completed, or they are developed in an illogical or unusual order. The schizophrenic inserts words or ideas in unexpected contexts, just as he enacts behavior which is inappropriate to the situation.

In psychosis, there are difficulties in maintaining a sense of temporal order, a disorientation and a loss of memory. There are evidences of projective phenomena such as delusions of persecution and hallucinations. The difficulties in logical order have given way to more dramatic aberrations in customary speech and thought (see Chapter 5).

A question then arises: Are there any disturbances of speech and thought which are characteristic of the least psychotic and non-psychotic states of schizophrenia? I think there are two such disorders, which I will mention here in relation to speech and content and later relate to behavior in general.

First, there is a difficulty in linearity in description, narration or exposition which is detectable in an interview. The patient uses strange or unusual ways to order the chronology of events. The sequence is not continuous, a problem we classically speak of as fragmentation. The patient is tangential, i.e., he takes off in one direction, then suddenly begins again and pursues another line of development. Also, the schizophrenic person seems to have difficulty remembering where the story is going, what point he is trying to reach.

Second, there may be deviations in the sense of spatial order. In a narrative, the schizophrenic is quite vague about who said what and who did this or that. In describing a place or a trip, it is quite unclear just what spaces lie next to each other and how the patient got from here to there. In explaining a dichotomy or an alternative of ideas, the patient does not use his hands to draw divisions and boundaries in the air as most people do, and if he does so we are likely to find these quite confusing. His problem with spatial order may be visible to us as well. The patient sits too far away for ordinary conversation, or else he sits much too close and looks and projects his voice to empty places in the room instead of to those who are present.

Clinicians have long noticed that schizophrenic people show deviations in the form of speech and have attributed these to disorders in thought or cognition. These thought disorders are traditionally characterized by abstractions such as "tangentiality," "circumstantiality" or "distractibility in attention." It is said, for instance, that the schizophrenic patient tries to tell of an experience but is distracted by other considerations, so that unexpected ideas creep into the exposition and produce an illogical sequence.

The structural linguist can record the speech of schizophrenic patients and spell out the exact deviations in syntax and sequential order for a given language. One can make analogous observations of the patterns of other task behavior, for schizophrenic people often "forget" what to do next when they are doing calculations or cooking a meal.

On the basis of structural analysis we can pinpoint some of the classical schizophrenic deviations in the ordering of behavior. We can say, for instance, that schizophrenic people sometimes violate the usual rules of syntactic order. We may notice that in a narration they do not carry out the usual sequences of ideation and stepwise exposition in accordance with the traditions of Aristotelian logic. In telling a story, a schizophrenic patient may relate the outcome of the theme somewhere in the middle of the narration. Or sometimes he brings in at step three or four an event which belongs to some other sort of story. Often he does not complete the sequence at all. Analogously, the schizophrenic may put the eggs on the plate before they are cooked or make an overt commitment to sexual intercourse before the preliminary steps of courtship have been accomplished.

These disorders in sequence and conclusion correspond to those which the clinician has observed in speech. They are all problems of linearity. This lack of linearity has been observed in borderline adolescents as a problem in accomplishing subjects in school which require linear effort. These include exposition, creative writing, reading and mathematics.

In Part I, I generalized that the schizophrenic person is also inept in his participation in face-to-face interactions. The pattern of this ineptness can be spelled out if a sufficient number of instances are observed. There are deviations in interpersonal distance, in the pattern of tactile contact and gaze. In part, these deviations can be attributed to disorders in sequencing. For instance, any participant in an interaction might use gaze avoidance if confronted with a stare of dominance or a display of sexuality early in a flirtation, but the schizophrenic person may use gaze avoidance before any such eventuality has developed. In fact, his eye avoidance may occur before the partners have even exchanged a greeting or taken face-to-face positions.

Many deviations in the structure of schizophrenic participation require different or additional explanations. These might be seen as actions which are inappropriate to the immediate, ongoing situation. A group of people are having what they consider an amiable conversation, but a paranoid group member suddenly takes offense and introduces a segment of behavior that ordinarily belongs to a hostile confrontation or a prizefight. In the middle of a serious interview, the schizophrenic participant suddenly smiles and makes an outrageously literal or metaphorical remark about the topic. Classic examples are the patient's response to the psychiatrist's question, "What brings you to the hospital?" Answer: "A taxicab." Or the interviewer asks if the patient's spouse is faithful, and the patient replies, "No, she cheats on her income tax." The psychodynamic clinician may have no difficulty in interpreting the motives and the unconscious significance of such "transcontextual" responses, but these interpretations do not explain away the deviation in structure. Whatever the meaning, the schizophrenic patient has violated the usual orders of action and context.

There is a variant in this problem of action and context that demands special mention in the study of schizophrenic patterns. The customary rules of social discourse require us to explain any unusual or deviant act of participation. At the least we apologize for it and demonstrate that we realize we have behaved in an uncustomary manner. The schizophrenic person often fails to do this, which is one basis for saying that there is a "lack of insight." Other schizophrenic people keep apologizing for the uncustomary behavior of other people, or they offer strange explanations for their own behavior. A well-known example is the paranoid's projection of blame, which may be followed by an elaborate exposition of persecutory motives and methods. Other examples might escape our conscious notice. For example, a schizophrenic woman at a party coughs, smiles and tells the assembled guests that she has a penis lodged in her throat. Again it is not difficult to imagine a psychodynamic explanation for her behavior, but we do not want to lose sight of the fact that a deviance in the relation of statement and context has been committed. This statement could be an "in house" joke among a group of psychoanalytic clinicians, but among relative strangers I would deem it typically schizophrenic.

There is another kind of example of deviation in action and context. A schizophrenic person often addresses people who are not present. The psychotic sits in a ward cupping his hands to better hear the voices; however, subtler examples can be seen in any interaction. The schizophrenic participant continually addresses gaze, hand gestures and remarks to an unfilled chair or an empty corner of the room. In Chapter 7 psychodynamic interpretations of these findings are reviewed and the findings are related to problems in the organization of neural systems.

Part III

Schizophrenia at
Suborganismic Levels

In the systems concept of levels, we usually recognize three levels of complexity below the level of the organism as a whole. These "suborganismic" levels are frequently designated as follows:

1) a level of organ systems (or physiological systems) such as the cardiovascular-renal, the musculo-skeletal, or the nervous system;

2) a level of cellular organizations and processes such as the systems of glomeruli of the kidneys, the organization of the adrenal medulla or the grey nuclei of the brain; and

3) a level of molecular processes such as the metabolic activities of neural conduction or the processes of biochemical transmission at the neural synapse.

In theory, we should now describe all of these subsystems and their activities in psychosis and schizophrenia, but there is reason to believe that disturbances in most of these are related to core-brain disruptions or the special life habits of many psychotic people in and out of institutions. On this account we can focus our study from here

103

on upon the central nervous system, provided we remember certain reservations.*

In previous decades this focus would mean that we would examine certain conceptions of psyche or mind. But a drastic change is taking place. An extensive revolution has occurred in the neurosciences, and some findings of extraordinary importance for our understanding of schizophrenia are emerging. A few elements of this revolution have received widespread attention, but the overall thrust of this shift is not generally understood even in the field of mental health.

If we are to make use of this development in the study of schizophrenia, we must understand the conceptions and findings of this radical shift in our paradigms of thought and method. Consequently, I will devote Chapter 7 to the changing scene before we get into the new views of schizophrenia at suborganismic levels.

---

* We must bear in mind that disturbances in any physiological subsystem are fed back to the central nervous system. Thus, physiological activities reverberate and sustain each other. We must also consider the possibility that metabolic dysfunctions within the central nervous system reflect general problems in nutrition and metabolism.

7

The Failures of Our Classical Paradigms

Classical neurology has not found the lesion or disorder in schizophrenia in spite of six generations of research. Classical psychologies have for four generations been unable to come up with a generally accepted formulation, nor have sociological theorists. When we consider the enormity of the problem of schizophrenia, we must face the fact that our classical paradigms* have suffered a serious failure.

There is another line of argument for this premise. We can now identify the neural problem in schizophrenia, but the new explanation has evolved only after an extensive revolution in the neurosciences. This revolution has already made the classical neurological paradigm obsolete, and it threatens to replace all of our classical psychologies.

In Chapter 8 I will discuss this revolution and spell out what has

---

* I will use Kuhn's definition of a paradigm (Kuhn, 1962). A paradigm is a way of looking at a particular class of phenomena—at stars or economics or at thought and behavior, for instance. It consists of a set of conceptual premises and a set of methods for confirming or denying these.

There are many theories within a paradigm. From time to time some of these are discredited by an experiment or a commonality of experience. But the set of premises, the way of thinking, is usually beyond the challenge of members of that science for generations or even for centuries. In psychiatry and mental health there are three coexisting paradigms today: a biological, a psychological and a sociological (see Part I). This is unusual, for ordinarily a new paradigm condemns the existing one to obsolescence, at least within the realm of that science.

been discovered at the level of neural systems in schizophrenia, but first let us look at the failures of our classical paradigms.

THE FRAGMENTATION OF THE PSYCHOLOGICAL PARADIGM

The psychological paradigm appeared about the turn of the twentieth century. In part it had its origins in the failure of neurology to present an adequate view of the central nervous system. It was not possible to relate observations of complex human behavior to a simple view of sensory and motor tracts. So theorists like Freud departed from an attempt to study the nervous system to the composition of metaphors and inferences about the psyche or mind.

Freud had been a neurologist. He regretted the postulation of a tripartite ego, id and superego view of neural anatomy and a libidinal and ego process view of neurophysiology. However, he saw no alternative if he were to have an explanatory system for his observations from psychosis and psychoanalysis. Pavlov (1979), and later the behaviorists, argued against a heuristic concept of mind, but apologies and arguments were to no avail. The psychological paradigm evolved, and it eventually enjoyed a reign of vast popularity. Having forgotten that mind and psyche were mere conceptions, whole generations of students came of age believing that ego and cognition were the realities of the human existence.

The Initial Split into Academic and Psychoanalytic Views

It is not uncommon in science to develop a hypothetical system to represent phenomena which cannot be visualized or studied directly. The history of astronomy reveals many examples, and the contemporary study of black holes and pulsars testifies to the fact that the processes of such deduction are still in vogue. Another example is found in the present state of subatomic physics. In view of the difficulties in comprehending the brain, there is nothing heretical about developing concepts of psyche or mind. There are, however, certain inevitable built-in problems in hypothetical systems, and the psychological paradigm has suffered from these since its inception.

When theorists deal with a conception about an aspect of nature, they can give free reign to their imaginations. Thus, there came to be as many versions of mind as there were theorists who could gain followings. Variants of the psychological paradigm multiplied in an almost endless profusion. Academic and experimental approaches, such as learning theory, behaviorism, neobehaviorism and cognitive theories, evolved. In the clinical tradition, psychoanalysis split into Freudian and many neo-Freudian versions and then into a series of psychodynamic approaches.

Although I will not even attempt to sketch the various views of schizophrenia which emerged in these many disciplines, I will delineate two popular conceptions which represent very different opinions.

Some Psychoanalytic Views. Freud (1949) formulated a metaphor that neatly predicts our most recent views of cortical-limbic-core-brain relationships. He stated that the ego was too weak in psychosis to prevent the emergence of id impulses. In the decades that followed, Freud's complex ideas of ego processes were reduced to the belief that the ego is a set of mechanisms of defense. These mechanisms include the denial of disturbing perceptions, the projection of blame and unwanted traits, and the incorporation or introjection of the activity patterns and traits of other people (A. Freud, 1946). In many contemporary psychoanalytic accounts of the schizophrenic problem, the characteristic ego deficiency is described in these terms, e.g., as a tendency to project one's own undesirable traits and motives to other people and to introject their esteemed qualities, thus perceiving these traits and motives of the self (Kernberg, 1968).

The psychoanalytic concept of ego weakness, therefore, embraces the idea that schizophrenic people cannot readily distinguish their own thoughts and motives from the thoughts of other people. In psychosis, the schizophrenic person may not be sure about which characteristics are his own and which belong to other people. These confusions in identity are often spoken of as blurring of the "ego boundaries." In family therapy versions of this idea, it is said that family members may have "undifferentiated egos" (Bowen, 1966).

Another conception of ego defense which figures in many psychodynamic concepts of schizophrenia is that termed "reaction formation," the tendency to overreact to one trait with its opposite. This approach explains the grandiosity of some schizophrenic patients as a reaction formation against feelings of inadequacy, which are engendered by overdependency, parental disdain and social failure. Grandiose overcompensations may also be fostered by parents who go to such lengths as explaining their child's rejection in school as a result of the jealousy of other children. We can conceive this problem as a vicious cycle. Inferiority is covered by grandiosity, which further adds to the child's inability to relate and learn. As a consequence, there is a further basis for inferiority feelings and another round of grandiosity and wish fulfillment.

The need to explain failure and overdependency may lead to another tack in schizophrenia. The child, as well as his relatives, may concoct archaic and fanciful explanations for failure and immaturity. Some of these are the heritage of ancient psychiatry itself, such as moonstruckness, demonic possession, or masturbation and diet. When the patient later repeats these explanations to psychiatrists, they are perceived as another example of bizarre conception. Each generation of science easily forgets the theories of earlier eras. This aspect of schizophrenia has been pursued in more cognitive language by Wynne (1970), who has studied bizarre cognitive patterns which are passed down in schizophrenic families (see Chapter 3).

Psychoanalytic theorists do attend to personality traits and their origins. Schizophrenic people are often characterized as narcissistic or orally regressive. In psychoanalytic concepts, these terms refer to overdependency, a failure of sexual maturation and the preoccupation with the self. These characterizations are less helpful than the concepts of Mahler and her associates (Mahler, 1958; Mahler and La Perriere, 1965) who actually observed mother-infant dyads in childhood schizophrenia and described autistic and symbiotic types of relationship. In fact, increasing attention has been given in psychoanalytic circles in the last 30 years to object relationships—particularly the mother-child relationship. Some of this literature has been cited in Chapter 4. One might also mention the studies of Winnicott (1953) on transitional objects to which the infant is attached in transition between the attachment to the mother and that to other people. Klein (1948) described a "paranoid" and a "depressive" position in infants which can be important in later psychosis. These and other psychoanalytic authors thus agree that schizophrenia is a failure of maturation.

Nevertheless, much of the psychoanalytic literature is based upon a much simpler notion—the idea that the behavior of schizophrenic people is simply an expression of their "underlying" feelings and thoughts. A large literature attributes schizophrenia to hatred of the mother or father, to dependent needs, to feelings of inadequacy, to latent homosexuality, to infantile cannibalistic needs and so on. Several psychoanalytic reviews of schizophrenia and additional concepts have been published (e.g., Sullivan, 1947; Federn, 1952; Fromm-Reichmann, 1950; Rosen, 1953; Bychowski, 1952; Arieti, 1974; Searles, 1955).

Cognitive and Experimental Approaches. In classical cognitive theory mental processes are abstracted as a sequence of steps, commonly termed perception, recognition, judgment and reasoning. The steps are usually studied by experimental procedures aimed at isolating the various steps of the processes. In most accounts, little or no attention is paid to the motor execution of cognitive processes. In fact, the great majority of experimental approaches in psychology avoid the term behavior. They jump instead to inferences about cognitive or mental events. Since all test responses are behaviors, this avoidance is almost absurd. It is also common in the various clinical disciplines to jump to inferences and avoid a statement about the behavior on which psychological inferences are based.* I will have more to say about this problem later. I will also mention a number of experimental approaches in Chapter 8.

A number of cognitive psychologists have attempted to provide a

---

* In classical psychiatry, patients speak and "have symptoms"; in psychoanalysis, they feel and reveal. In experimental and cognitive psychology, they simply respond. In behaviorism and behavioral modification, people have been known to walk and otherwise move, but they usually just have responses and symptoms; and in the humanistic psychologies, patients feel and express.

These terms are a matter of loyalty and disciplinary membership. A psychoanalyst or a humanist who used the word "behavior" might become suspect as a spy from behavior mod. A psychoanalyst who said someone "behaved" would be a revisionist in the direction of superficiality, while a Skinnerian who allowed that people feel would be unscientific, and so on and so on.

view of mental processes in structural or field terms, i.e., to provide
a view of form and pattern. Tolman (1948) introduced the concept
of cognitive maps, and Lewin (1951) described a theory of "cognitive
structure." More recently, a picture of cognitive images and of plans
for motor execution have been provided in the cognitive tradition
(Miller, Galanter and Pribram, 1960). This and other recent cognitive studies will concern us later in detail, for they have played a
major role in the neuro-systems revolution and the emergence of a
new "neuropsychological" paradigm.

Further Fragmentation of the Psychodynamic Approach

There were always some serious difficulties with the psychoanalytic
version of the psychological paradigm. Like the other conceptual
systems of psychology, it ignored the behavior on which its inferences
were based, and its inferences were about a conception of the nervous
system instead of being about the nervous system itself. Nevertheless,
psychoanalysis was a cohesive discipline with a tight methodology
until the 1940s. Then it began to fragment into multiple social-
psychological and other versions. This was not merely a fragmentation into Freudian and neo-Freudian schools of thought; rather the
more integrated idea of psychodynamic processes was recast into a
myriad of simple expression theories.

Maybe I can best explain what I mean by this assertion with a
rather typical, contemporary case history.

Charlie is an unusually bright and charming Irish-American who
had his first psychotic break while he was a college freshman. The
family reluctantly agreed to family therapy, but they refused to
attend sessions after about two months. Then Charlie began individual therapy in a private practice, but after a year he had another
psychotic break, and the family claimed they had no more funds for
private therapy. At that point Charlie was referred to our clinic.

Charlie was the favorite client of the clinic. He supported all the
program, he did favors for the other patients and the staff members.
But when Charlie got psychotic, he was difficult. He insulted and
threatened everyone and disrupted the whole clinic routine. Worse
than this, everyone liked him so much that it depressed the whole

place to see him break down. All in all, four staff members had worked intensively with Charlie, but he got psychotic more often now, and he stayed psychotic longer. He was kept on larger and larger doses of phenothiazines, and he was beginning to show a tardive dyskinesia.

We had many staff meetings on what to do about Charlie. Let me tell you about one of them. Mary, one of his ex-therapists, said that Charlie's mother was such a bitch that she drove him to psychosis. She said we had to find a foster home for him. Joe said it was impossible to separate them. Then he added, "Even if we did, he hates her so much that he'd stay schizophrenic to get even with her." Tom didn't agree with that. He blamed Charlie's passive father and thought Charlie had a deep-seated oedipal attachment to his mom. Clara said this was nonsense. She thought Charlie had to react hostilely to prove he was masculine. She thought Charlie had a basic passivity and maybe some latent homosexual trends. The psychiatrist didn't agree with this. He said Clara had the problem upside down. He said he thought Charlie had to be passive to cover up his oral-sadistic impulses and his murderous aggression.

No agreement was ever reached about Charlie's underlying dynamics. We did agree to make a home visit and to try again to bring the family together for a session. I'll tell you about that a little later. In the meantime, let's ask what problem leads to such a diversity in staff opinion.

The Problem of an Expressional Model. There is one thing every staff member did agree upon. It was implicitly agreed that Charlie was expressing *some* emotion, conflict or need. This is the general belief in psychodynamic circles today. The disagreement is about which force of a myriad of possibilities is being expressed.

When we analyze this problem in conceptual or methodological terms, this degree of disagreement makes sense. It is an inevitable consequence of the current bankruptcy of the psychological paradigm. *It seems that thousands of us actually believe that the human existence is so simple that we can account for it by a model of expression,* by a notion that *something* is being expressed. Once we believe this, we can have recourse to a hundred lists of needs, drives, conflicts or emotions. To know what is "wrong" with Charlie (or anyone else), then, we need only reach into the deck and pull out the ascription which was advocated by our favorite teacher or author.

From time to time in the history of science, a revolutionary new paradigm has emerged and swept its predecessor into obsolescence. We do not know all of the reasons for such cycles, but on historical grounds we can say this: Just before a new paradigm emerges, the previous one is in a state of fragmentation, with multiple conflicting viewpoints.

If I am correct that this is the state of affairs in many psychodynamic circles today, then not only are we primed for a conceptual revolution, but we also badly need one. As I will say later, it is already upon us. Those who have a vested interest in one brand of contemporary psychodynamics are in for a tough time. In academic psychology, the house is in no better order. In addition, there are S-R, learning theory, behavioral and neobehavioral schools; there are cognitive, gestalt and other versions of individual psychology and many schools of social psychology. We can take little consolation in being the last science to be overidden by a conceptual revolution in the twentieth century. The physical sciences have suffered three conceptual revolutions in this century. Biology has had a social and a molecular revolution since the 1940s. The wave of new thinking which is now threatening the old psychological paradigm has radically altered sociology, economics, anthropology, neurophysiology and biochemistry.*

Later on I will try to say what this new wave of thought is about. Now we should step back and ask a prior question: What is the problem with the psychological paradigm that it suffers from such simplistic reductions and endless fragmentations?

PROBLEMS OF THE PSYCHOLOGICAL PARADIGM

So far I have focused on one problem of the psychological paradigm, i.e., on its fragmentation and its warring doctrinal divisions.

---

* Many will think I am referring here to the changes in psychology and psychiatry which followed the introduction of social perspectives and interaction theory. These are mistakenly viewed in clinical circles as "systems theories." If you believe interaction theory in family or group therapy is systems theory, if you think these changes have been radical, wait until you see what is coming next.

But analogous failures have plagued neurology and the biological paradigm in their applications to schizophrenia. Nor has the sociological paradigm answered our theoretical or clinical problems in the area of schizophrenia. These failures will be considered later in this chapter; for the moment, I will keep the focus on the psychological disciplines for a tactical reason. If we understand the problems of the psychological paradigm, we can more readily make a criticism of all of the classical paradigms as they relate to the problem of schizophrenia.

I think two problems of conception (or epistemology) have been built into the psychological paradigm *from the beginning*. Collectively, these have made its fragmentation inevitable and demanded its eventual replacement.

In the doing of science we hope to be able to observe a system directly. Then we can hear and see and feel it and say how it works. Since the nervous system is not directly observable to us in its living state, we must use inferential methods. We must examine what goes into the system and what comes out of it and then try to infer what processes must occur to explain the transformations. This way of doing science is always subject to debate about the unseen processes, and divisions in thought are likely unless all theorists ascribe to a discipline of an unchallenged authority. This was the case in psychoanalysis for a while. There are, however, two errors of method which can doom an inferential science to a nightmare of multiple conceptions and endless doctrinal warfare.

The Fallacy of Reduced and Unstated Data. The validity of an inferential science depends upon the careful description of the data base and its context. The data for inferences about the nervous system (or the mind) are observations of the ongoing experience and of the behavioral outputs. In the case of people, the ongoing experience is a complex system of events, and the outputs are mainly the bodily states and the motor activities. It is true that we can now measure some metabolic end products in the cerebrospinal fluid, and we can record electroencephalographic waves. But in the main, the responses are *what the subject or patient says and does*.

Freud repeatedly warned us that the psychodynamics of the patient required us to view the ongoing life situation *and* the past life experience in the light of complex patterns of activity. For example, he made this point clearly in his analysis of the three "legs" or contexts of the dream, i.e., the "residues of the previous day, the past experience and the relation to the therapist." In other language, Pavlov (1979), too, warned us about the complexity of the S-R relationship. But the warning has not been heeded. The experimentalist is usually willing to flash a light or a card and call that *the* stimulus. He ignores the laboratory, the relationship, and the life situation at the time of the experiment. Rosenthal (1976) has shown us that what the experimenter says *and how he says it* will noticeably influence the outcome of an experiment in psychology. I cannot see that Rosenthal's finding has made a great deal of difference in experimental psychology.

The clinician is not likely to be any more attentive to the complexity of contexts. He is likely to boil down a complex experience to some abstracted notion. Maybe it was Mom's possessiveness or Dad's inattention. Maybe Charlie got psychotic because he flunked math. The expression theorists do not even bother to recognize the possibility of a stimulus or a life situation. In their book, the patient simply expresses an "inside" emotion or some other kind of "intrapsychic" force.

The reduction of the data for inference is not only a problem on the input side of the ledger. The experimental subject is supposed to pick a card or push a button. As he does so, he does a hundred other things too, but the experimentalist notes only the formal response, and when he publishes his paper, he will do no more than count the button pushes. Then he will jump to an inference about the alleged psychological process which accounts for the response.

The clinician will not tell us about behavior either. In a case report, he will tell us the age, sex and diagnosis, but he will not say what the patient looks like or describe the cultural background. If you ask a student therapist such questions at a case presentation, he will probably not be able to say. Sometimes the case report will tell us a little of what the client says, but it will tell us nothing else about his behavior. We will be told only what inferences the clinician has made about the patient's mental processes.

Let me summarize this point as briefly as possible. We have a strategy of science which depends upon a careful description of situations and behavioral patterns, *but we have virtually no data base.* At worst we have nothing but papers and books full of inferences; at best we have a reductive view of *"the* stimulus" and *"the* response" or of *the* upsetting factor and *the* stated emotional response.

In the last generation, a valiant effort was made to give these approaches a quasi-scientific front. Judges were asked to pass on clinical inferences, and elaborate statistics were carried out to determine the correlation of their judgments. But no amount of statistics can prove the validity of an inference, and a consensus is only a measure of reliability within a particular doctrine. Fifty million Frenchmen can be wrong, and the objections of a hundred million American fundamentalists do not demolish the value of Darwin's work on evolution. In short, *a psychological inference, in the absence of a careful analysis of situation and behavior patterns, is nothing more than a recitation of doctrinal belief.* Not only do we lack a data base in the psychological sciences, but even the word "behavior" is treated as a verboten term. Even the behaviorists abstract "the symptoms" of schizophrenia.

Aristotelianization of Constructs. There is also a tradition in formal Western thought which further narrows our ability to see situations and behavior patterns in a comprehensive way. It also narrows our ability to make inferences. This mode of thinking is often attributed to Aristotle,* so it can be termed "Aristotelian." In this mode of conception, all phenomena are believed to have *a* cause, which is believed to emanate from some person, thing or place. This mode is so entrenched that theorists make up imaginary causative things or places and imaginary forces when they deal with any conception of nature. As a consequence, various psychological thinkers have selected a causative stimulus or force in the mind or nervous system. The mind was said to have parts such as the ego, the superego and

---

* Aristotle once recommended that we study complex phenomena by reducing them to their essence or main component. He then opined that the main component of a phenomenon is some physical component which may act as a causative agent.

In the logical positivism which has dominated experimental science, the term "Aristotelian" implies an armchair scientist who does no actual observing. All of these reductions of Aristotle are quite unfair, for he was a thorough naturalistic observer, and he left us 33 surviving volumes in which he expressed quite different views. Maybe Aristotle, like Freud and other great thinkers, could not bear to throw away the material he wrote on his bad days.

the id. The ego was depicted like a little person who got weak or strong, sick or well, and capable or incapable of controlling the id and making decisions. In all versions of psychology, behavior was explained by composing a list of instinctual forces, drives, needs or motives.

In time, the metaphors and conceptions of a hypothetical system became more real to its workers than the natural system they were supposed to represent. To those who worked in the psychological paradigm, the ego or the will or the cognitive structure became more real than the brain or the nervous system. This was not only a matter of realness. To many psychological thinkers, the constructs of their doctrines were superior to a view of neural organization. It became more profound (deeper) and more humanistic to think, for example, about emotions and thoughts than about the body or the nervous system. In the long run, the refusal to bother with the patterns of situations and behavior and the reductionism to place and cause resulted in an almost infinite set of guesses about the essence of the human experience and the cause of schizophrenia.

THE DEMISE OF CLASSICAL NEUROSCIENCE

Almost the same fate overtook classical neurology and the sciences of neurophysiology and neurochemistry. Neurologists and neuropathologists kept looking for the lesions of schizophrenia; neurophysiologists kept studying the nerve or the neurone in isolation. And each year some neurochemist found a suspicious discoloration on the paper of chromotography and claimed that he had at last found the cause of schizophrenia.

As I will describe in Chapter 8, these reductive efforts have been replaced by integrative efforts because the revolution of field and systems has already reordered the neurosciences. However, the problem still plagues clinical neurology, especially when it comes to cases of schizophrenia. To further demonstrate this problem, let me begin once again with a representative case history.

Mr. and Mrs. Smith had a son in his late teens who acted a little strange and didn't look quite right. He didn't seem energetic or interested in anything; his school marks were high in music appreciation, but he was failing in mathematics and physical education. The Smiths didn't take any action, though, until they got a call from the school psychologist. She told them that Joey wasn't doing well in school. In addition to his obviously low marks, he didn't pay attention in class and didn't socialize well. She had done a test battery on him which showed normal verbal scores and some potential artistic interest, but he did not read well or do mathematics adequately. His school behavior seemed to show a problem in judgment and an inability to carry out assignments and plans. On a sorting test, he had some problems with items and categories, and in interview he was remote, guarded and circumstantial. She suggested a possible learning disorder; she suspected that he was a borderline schizophrenic, but she did not state this.

They had a family conference and decided to take Joey to the family doctor because he didn't look very healthy. He was sallow and listless but also seemed tense and anxious. The family doctor agreed that Joey didn't look very healthy, although an examination and a battery of laboratory tests were negative. His assessment was that the problem was probably functional, but in order to make sure, he sent Joey to a neurologist. He either did not want to say that he suspected schizophrenia, or he did not recognize the problem in this way.

The neurologist did a careful examination and found no disorder of motor function or sensation. Joey could see well and hear well when he paid attention, and he had an adequate perception of touch, pinprick, vibration and the position of his toes and fingers. If there was a nuerological problem, it was cortical, but there was no evidence of increased intracranial pressure on examination of the eye grounds and no epileptic phenomena which could indicate an irritating mass of the cerebral cortex. The neurologist then reasoned as follows: This is probably a functional disorder, but it is my job to rule out a lesion in the silent areas of the cerebral cortex, i.e., in those areas such as the frontal poles and the temporal lobe which do not show neurological signs. He queried Joey more carefully. Did Joey have any trouble seeing? No. The neurologist tested vision and the visual fields. Did Joey have any sensations of things growing larger or smaller? No. Was there any history of having seen or heard familiar scenes when Joey was alone? No, except that Joey had several days of such visions years ago when he had a high fever with chicken pox. And he used to have a lot of nightmares, which lasted after he woke up. The neurologist had to assume that there was no evidence of a gross lesion of the temporal lobes. Then he had Joey feel coins with his eyes closed. Joey could tell a quarter from a nickel without any trouble. There was no evidence of a lesion of the parietal areas of the cortex. There is no clinical test of the frontal areas unless the lesion has moved back to the motor area. The motor system was normal. The neurological examination was negative. Joey's family argued: Why did Joey lack concentration? Why wasn't he ever hungry? He had no interest in girls and was so pale and tense.

The neurologist reconsidered. Was it possible Joey had a craniopharyngioma or a lesion of the core-brain, of the hypothalamus, for instance—not likely. The tracts for motor activity and cerebral balance run next to the core-brain, and a tumor above the pituitary might reveal itself in a narrowing of the visual fields. He would take no chances; he ordered skull X-rays and a careful test of the visual fields. All were negative. Joey was referred to a psychotherapist, who assumed that Joey is a borderline schizophrenic. Joey began psychotherapy but quit after three sessions.

The neurologist had several problems in assessing Joey. There was no mass lesion impinging upon testable functions. In spite of Joey's tenseness, the problem seemed to be a deficiency of function, but there was no detectable focal destruction of brain tissue. There was nothing wrong with the sensory or motor tracts.* There was a vague impression of cortical and corebrain dysfunction, but there are no standard clinical tests to determine where or what this was. We

---

* Some clinicians have observed that many schizophrenic people are physically awkward. Possibly awkwardness reflects a lack of social experience, a good deal of motor inhibition and a measure of lifelong ambivalence about what actions to take. In any event, all schizophrenic people are not awkward, and a motor or neuromuscular problem is not characteristic of schizophrenia. I recently watched five very psychotic young men, all on phenothiazines, represent their hospital in a baseball game with a team from an alcoholic rehabilitation center. The schizophrenic team won handily, and it was amazing to observe the rigidity which they all showed from phenothiazines disappear with motor engagement.

will have to go to the frontiers of structural science to learn about them.

Unless Joey's neurologist had had an untraditional or recent background in neuroanatomy and neurophysiology, he was likely to have another problem. He was likely to think that the brain was made up of hundreds of discrete grey nuclei and forty some discrete areas of cerebral cortex which lie like a mosaic of tile on the surface of the brain. From the standpoint of neuroanatomy, such discrete areas do exist, but all of them are interconnected. They do not function as separate places, each of which "gives off" its own function. But we did not realize this until the last 30 years or so. Instead, we had an Aristotelian view of separate Brodmann's areas of separate nuclei, and we expected to somehow test each one to find a disorder. In other words, neurology, like psychiatry and psychology, was once a science of focus responses and items of activity.

THE PROBLEM OF SOCIAL PSYCHOLOGY AND THE SOCIOLOGICAL PARADIGM

This chapter is already overly arduous, and we are all tired of critiques, so I will be brief about the shortcomings of the sociological paradigm as it has been applied to the problems of psychology and psychiatry. Almost two generations ago the social-psychological approaches of pioneers such as G. H. Mead (1934) and H. S. Sullivan (1953) were applied to psychological research and to clinical problems such as schizophrenia. There is no doubt that these views have enriched our understanding. For example, a social perspective of the processes of maturation has led us to such concepts as symbiosis and a clearer view of the family relationships of the child who will be schizophrenic. In addition, group and family therapies and the increasing practice of convening a social network for psychotic people have greatly improved our therapeutic regimes.

Nevertheless, I think that the social perspective has been watered down so much that it has not had its potential impact. Society has been conceived of as a thing or an agent of simple causation. In this sophomoric view, it is held that schizophrenia is caused by the society or the medical profession, as if there were nothing more to the story (see Part I). More commonly, the processes of reduction have involved a psychologization of social perspectives, i.e., making them fit existing psychological models. In clinical circles, social "factors" are added to our lists of the cause of schizophrenia and, in the laboratory, the social situation is just one more stimulus.

More About the Case of Charlie. Maybe I can illustrate what I mean by a few more fragments from the case of Charlie. After the clinic staff had met, a few of us arranged to visit Charlie's home, and we set up a series of family sessions. When we visited the home, we did a tour of the house with Charlie as a willing guide. He showed us the house layout and where everyone in the family slept, ate and talked. We discovered some new angles on Charlie's psychosis that I would not be willing to list simply as another cause or stimulus.

Charlie was the middle one of eleven children of a well-to-do suburban family. All of Charlie's siblings had left home for employment, college or marriage. There were four bedrooms on the second floor and four on the third of the large home. The parents occupied a master bedroom on the second floor. In spite of all the other empty rooms, Charlie lived in the smallest bedroom on the third floor. Across the hall lived a very psychotic, older female boarder who had lived there for many years and who had acted as an "aunt" or second mother to Charlie, but who had never been mentioned in all of the family sessions. Although she had been Charlie's closest companion for many years, all members of the family tried to deny her existence. I am sure we would never have learned of her, even from Charlie, had we not made a home visit.

The discovery of this woman's existence led to a family admission. She had raised Charlie while the mother raised the other ten children. This should have markedly changed the staff's theory of the real mother as a "schizophrenogenic mother." In fact, it changed no opinions at all, for good theories are not to be disrupted by data.

We made another interesting discovery on the home visit. Charlie was said to have become psychotic at college after he smoked a lot of pot. But in fact, Charlie became psychotic when he walked into his bedroom during Thanksgiving recess of his first year of college. On the walls of his bedroom he had collected for years a montage of photographs of people with piercing eyes. When he left for college, his mother took them down and threw them away. When Charlie came home and discovered this, he went into a psychotic rage. (This issue will concern us again in Chapter 8.)

The first family session after the home visit was not unusual. Mother was surly and only answered direct questions. Father seemed reluctant to talk at all, but he backed up Mother's assertions. In the main, Mother blamed Charlie's psychosis on pot-smoking and the wrong crowd at college. When Charlie occasionally tried to confront his mother, she glared at him, and his head and voice dropped in silence (see Chapter 4). Otherwise, no family member looked at or addressed another. Nevertheless, Charlie moved in synchrony with each parent as that parent talked (see Chapter 4).

On the way back to the clinic, Mary said the session confirmed her opinion. The mother was a domineering bitch, and that's why Charlie had so much trouble. Tom blamed the father's passivity. The experience had not produced any change in the simple formulations which had been voiced at the staff meeting. The social perspective had produced only a conceptual system of blame.

At the second and last session, the parents announced their unwillingness to continue with future sessions. During the meeting, the mother reiterated her charge that pot had damaged Charlie's brain. She said Charlie had always been an angry, passive and withdrawn child. The father did not quite agree. We wondered if they had somehow shortchanged Charlie. At the end of the session, Charlie's father turned to me and asked, "Do you think schizophrenia is a social or a psychological or biological condition?" I ask you, colleague, do you think it's sociological, psychological *or* biological?

Interactionalism and the Loss of the Social Perspecitve

Mary and Tom had blamed the parents. This approach shows a typical misconception of social perspective. Society is somehow "out there." It is an enemy, impinging upon us. On this account, we and our clients are somehow not part of society or the troubles it brings us.

But a psychological perspective loses much more understanding of social processes. Communication and social participation are characteristically viewed as expressions of the participants' feelings, motives or personalities. To be sure, people do show feelings and traits in an interaction which color their participation. But when we view the participant's psychology as the cause of the interaction, we lose sight of two valuable aspects of social process. First of all, human relationships are made up of behaviors. This is the medium through which we communicate. Concepts of affect or motive are inferences that we make about the manner of participation. When we focus upon them, we miss a view of the interaction itself. My other point is that people participate in social process. They take part in activities as old as their culture—sometimes as old as our species. If we view the participants as making the process or doing it to each other or being to blame for it, we miss a view of the process itself. In either case, we have no data base for our guesses.

All in all, I think the psychologicalization of social processes has cost us three sorts of valuable information. These are 1) a view of the forms or patterns of human events; 2) a view of cultural differences; and 3) a view of home life, for home life is not what is said in the office. Whenever we build down a perspective, we lose priceless information. It is rather like going to the ballgame just to eat a hot dog.

8

The Schizophrenic Problem

in Cerebral Organization

In this chapter I will review the emergence of a new view of the *organization* of neural subsystems and the *structure* of behavior. After I have sketched the new paradigm and the conceptual framework in which it has emerged, I will review the data and point out that, at this level, *schizophrenia is a relative disorganization in the relations of cortical areas in both hemispheres and also a loss of the regulatory function of the limbic and corebrain systems.* I will close with a theory of degrees of further disorganization in psychosis and make a few comments about the contexts of these disorganizations.

THE NEUROSCIENCE REVOLUTION

A few of the discoveries about brain hormones, namely, the neurotransmitters and endorphins, have received wide attention, but it is not generally known that the neuroscience revolution has occurred at multiple levels of organization. It invokes a different approach even to the study of organismic behavior. It is producing a new, unified view of the nervous system as a whole and allows an understanding of the organization and process of maturation of cellular fields in the grey matter of the brain. In other words, it is a revolution in macro-physiology of the nervous system, as well as in brain metabolism and neural synapses.

There is another aspect of this revolution which is not widely understood. It not only involves the discovery of new instruments and methodologies for the study of the brain, but also causes a radical shift in the whole concept of how to do science as well. It is this shift in the epistemology of science that I would like to describe first.

The Epistemological Shift

Periodically in the history of science, a new paradigm will evolve. Earlier I defined a paradigm as a body of theories, methods and findings about a *particular* phenomenon (Kuhn, 1962). A new paradigm revolutionizes a given science. An epistemology is much broader than a paradigm, for it is a way of thinking about all phenomena, about all of nature. Accordingly, an epistemological shift is much less common in the history of a society. In fact, one can argue that we have not had a radical epistemological shift in Western civilization since the days of Aristotle and Plato.

We are experiencing one now, however, and we have been for a long time. Possibly it dates as far back as Darwin, who shifted from a view of immutable forms to a view of evolution, change through time. Certainly, the new epistemology is evident in Einsteinian field theory and relativity. The thrust of this epistemological change appeared again in the 1940s as general systems theory and cybernetics.

The field sciences move in an integrative direction. They seek to depict processes and relations between them and to come up with a view of the field of events *as a whole*. In contrast to the previous epistemology of Aristotelian thought, they do not reduce complex phenomena in order to find a main part or causative agent. Consider a specific example. In the nineteenth century, the doctrine of materialism became ascendant in science and remained so until very recently. In this version of the old epistemology, it was held that we understood things when we could see their elementary physical components, so the materialists tried to reduce life to the study of atoms or particles. In systems theory, we would today insist that the nature of living systems arises from the *organization* of their elements.

This shift in the very direction of study has characterized the neuro-science revolution. Previously, the focus in neurophysiology was on the activity of the single neuron, but now one emphasis is upon neural conductivity across the synaptic junction. In former years we studied the neuronal composition of grey nuclei, while now we try to visualize the relation between nuclei and tracts. We speak now of continuous functional columns which extend almost the length of the central nervous system. Whereas we used to focus on the ascending sensory and the descending motor pathways of the nervous system, we now visualize the relation of many other neural subsystems.

The Emergence of a Structural Paradigm

With this epistemological shift, a new paradigm has gradually evolved in the sciences of behavior and the brain. Its earliest manifestations were almost contemporary with Einstein's applications in astronomy. I am referring to the gestalt view of perception (Wertheimer, 1925; Koffka, 1935), Sapir's (1921) evolution of structural linguistics, or, for another early example, Lewin's (1951) development of a psychological field theory and a concept of the *structure* of cognition.

The new paradigm really came into its own later on. It surfaced in the late 1940s in anthropology, as in the study of *patterns* of culture (Benedict, 1946), and gained strength from the study of communication about 1960 when the patterning of participation and the order of interactional events began to be emphasized (Birdwhistell, 1970; McQuown et al., 1971; Scheflen, 1963, 1974; Bateson, 1972; Kendon, 1977). This emerging paradigm has no generally accepted name, so I will give it one. I will call it the "structural paradigm" because in each of its versions the emphasis is upon the form, pattern or structure.

Unfortunately, few researchers in the structure of motor behavior have paid attention to the phenomena of schizophrenia. In Chapters 4 and 6, I reviewed a few findings about schizophrenic participation in an interaction. In Chapter 6, I concluded that schizophrenic people show a failure to accomplish traditional linear sequences and an inability to relate items to contexts. Now a large body of structural research is accumulating in several related areas of cognition and neurophysiology. Miller, Galanter and Pribram (1960) published a milestone volume describing cognitive structure. Pribram published an extensive review on the integration of cognitive and neurophysiological findings in the structure of neural systems activities. And Jaynes (1976) has written a documentation of historical records on the state of the mind three centuries ago.

THE SCHIZOPHRENIC PROBLEM IN CEREBRAL INTEGRATION

There is mounting evidence that the schizophrenic person has two interrelated problems in organizing the activities of the forebrain. Suppose we take them up one at a time.

The Problem of the Dominant Hemisphere

Ornstein (1977) has marshalled evidence that "normal" people integrate complicated linear activities with the use of the cerebral hemisphere in which the functions of speech are well developed. In most people this is the left cerebral hemisphere. In fact, Ornstein used the term "left cerebral dominance" to describe people who could perform linear activities with great skill.

Such performance requires the following activities to be coordinated: images or memories must be evoked, a set of steps must be remembered, and an image of achievement, i.e., a picture of the finished task, must be recalled. In addition, there must be a temporary or relative inhibition of distracting sensory inputs and a control of corebrain upheavals. Then a plan can be conceived and put into execution with motor activities. In neurophysiological terms, the activities of all areas of the cerebral cortex must be drawn into this effort. To be more specific, the occipital and superior temporal cortex maintain visual and auditory images, the parietal cortex stores kinesthetic memories and an "image of achievement," the frontal poles seem to be important in sequential memory, and the frontal cortex also organizes patterns of motor behavior. The details of these assertions have been described by Pribram (1971).

My inference is clear. *The schizophrenic person's relative inability to accomplish linear tasks suggests some problem in the integration of these activities.* It is most likely a problem in integrating cerebral activities in the dominant hemisphere. But we must be careful, for there are several reservations we must make. The acquisition of these abilities is an accomplishment of at least all of childhood and adolescence—an accomplishment that is schooled in an industrial society. A relative inadequacy is not a sign of disease or organic lesion. Furthermore, its attainment has a social context; it depends upon an absence of fatigue, drug intoxication and illness. There is more to the story even at the level of neural systems. The ability to do linear tasks requires a temporary inhibition of corebrain activities and an integration of cortical activity between the left and right cerebral hemispheres. This is not, however, an Aristotelian approach; we are not dealing with a place or "source" of the problem.

The Problem of Bilateral Hemispheric Integration

The non-language hemisphere, usually the right one, is apparently employed in such activities as facial recognition, the recognition of spatial order and the reproduction of broad gestalten. Ornstein (1977), for example, points out that architects and artists are often "right-brain dominant." Those who think in simple dichotomies have already taken to calling artists "right-brained," while they speak of those who have linear task abilities as "left-brained." The implication is that some people use one cerebral hemisphere, while other people employ the other one. Nothing could be more reductive or sophomoric. The integration of any complex activity involves both an ability at visualizing the gestalten of contexts and the ability to plan and carry out a linear production. Everyday living and work require an integration of left- and right-brain activity.

Anatomically, this integration must be carried out by means of the interhemispheric pathways of the corpus callosum and the anterior commissure. Neurophysiologically, it may be accomplished by a rapid oscillation of mutual inhibition (Sugerman et al., 1971; Kinsbourne, 1975). In schizophrenia, there may be a delay in this process. Sugerman et al. (1971) report that the phasic alternation in activity between hemispheres in schizophrenic subjects is delayed fourfold.

There is already a massive literature on the subject of cerebral laterality. Many articles describe how cerebral integration is tested, how it is affected by the destruction of the corpus callosum and how it is impaired in depression and schizophrenia. This literature has been thoroughly reviewed in a recent paper by Wexler (1980), so I will mention only a few examples in relation to schizophrenia. Gur (1978) showed that non-schizophrenic people show a superiority in spatial recognition with right hemisphere and a superiority in verbal recognition with the left, while schizophrenic subjects showed a superiority in both abilities by the *right* hemisphere. Beaumont and Diamond (1973) demonstrated a relative decrease in ability by the left hemisphere in a letter-matching task. On the electroencephalogram, schizophrenic patients apparently have a higher proportion of alpha activity over the left temporal lobe, while non-schizophrenic controls have a higher proportion on the right (Urstad, 1979). This is presumed to mean a relatively lower proportion of conscious-directed activity.

So go the data in report after report in the new approach to cerebral dominance and cerebral interaction. Blau (1977) has produced a startling statistic about the relationship of schizophrenia and a failure of left cerebral dominance. The tendency to draw circles in a clockwise direction is called torque. (Most Americans draw circles in a counterclockwise direction.) Torque is believed to indicate an inadequate left cerebral dominance. Blau (1977) found a statistically higher incidence of schizophrenia ten years later in a group of children who had shown torque when they were about five years old. There seems to be little doubt that schizophrenic people have difficulty in left cerebral integration and in the integration of left and right cerebral interaction. My belief about the matter is this: If the schizophrenic cannot adequately integrate hemispheric functions, he might have difficulty in relating verbal and other specific task behaviors to the spatial and other contexts in which he is to act. If so, the new research confirms the impression we have derived from communicational participation, the older lines of laboratory inquiry and clinical experience of the inappropriateness of schizophrenic behavior to ongoing situations. In short, there is a *problem in unit-context relations, and this problem appears to be reflected in tests of cerebral integration and hemispheric interaction.**

Corebrain Subsystems

In the dorsal portion of the corebrain and brainstem, there is a continuous column of grey matter which conducts information about the physiological and metabolic state of the body. This subsystem regulates the "internal environment" of the body. There is also a continuous grey column called the "reticular activating system," which is also under the regulation of the limbic system. It acts as a "thermostat" for degrees of arousal, alertness and consciousness. It modulates sensory inputs to the cortex and is in turn modulated by the cortex by way of the limbic system.

The corebrain also establishes parameters for such activities as fight and flight, appetite, thirst and sexual arousal (see Chapter 5).

In the non-psychotic states of schizophrenia, there is usually a hypoactivity in most of these subsystems, though in many paranoid personalities without overt psychosis, the opposite states appear. In deviations in the hypoactive direction, "appetites" are low, arousal or alertness is reduced, and bodily tonus is flaccid. In the hyperactive direction, the opposite states appear. There is hyperarousal, more active fiight and flight reactions, and so forth. *In either case, there is a disturbance in the modulation of corebrain subsystems,* i.e., there is too great or too little control and inhibition. It is possible to explain this failure of modulation by postulating an insufficient or excessive temporal lobe and cortical activation (via the limbic system). It is possible, for example, that in non-psychotic states of schizophrenia, an excessive degree of concentration is required to

---

* There is a reservation I have about these findings and postulates. The researchers who specialize in tests of cerebral function make much of the distinction between left cerebral dysfunctions and dysfunction in the integration between hemispheres. I have also made a distinction between the problem of linearity and the problem of event-context relations. It may be that they are in fact clearly distinguishable in test interpretations or clinical observation, but the difference may be overplayed. A disorder in either hemisphere could easily disorder hemispheric integration. I suggest we keep the distinction for the time being, since it is already traditional, and it will help us to distinguish stages of schizophrenic psychoses.

maintain organized, linear behavior or cerebral dominance. This may produce an exceptional measure of limbic inhibition upon corebrain functions.

In summary, then, we can make an educated guess that the following situation usually prevails in the non-psychotic states of schizophrenia. There is a relative deficit in the ability to maintain linearity and event-context relations (or left cerebral dominance and hemispheric integration). This requires an extraordinary (but relatively unsuccessful) effort to limit sensory inputs and exercise excessive limbic inhibition. However, this state of neural subsystems is unstable. In certain situations the schizophrenic person is prone to a breakdown in this uneasy equilibrium; a psychotic episode occurs.

There are many such situations. One may be the loss of the dependent state and of input of organizing cues and commands, as was allegedly the case 3000 years ago in the bicameral era which Jaynes (1976) has described.

PSYCHOTIC DISORGANIZATION AND SOME OF ITS CONTEXTS

In Chapter 5, I sketched four degrees of psychotic disorganization from a clinical perspective. I will postulate now that these are associated with degrees of disintegration in the relations of neural subsystems. I will point out that these have contexts too.

So far, I have written about the non-psychotic states of schizophrenia. I have argued that people with this dysfunction suffer an inability to sequence and complete cognitive and physical tasks and have difficulty in relating actions (and thought) to their usual contexts. Then I added that this problem is sustained by social situations and by ideas and behaviors that we can abstract in psychological terms.

Psychosis of the First Order

We must conceptualize this relative inability described above from two sides of the issue. There is a deficit in these functions which becomes observable when the schizophrenic person is called upon to complete certain tasks or participate in certain interactions. On the other hand, a degree of linear ability and context-correct behavior can be sustained in favorable social situations. In the newer metaphors, the non-psychotic schizophrenic can sustain a measure of cerebral dominance and hemispheric integration in a sustaining situation. *In psychotic disorganizations of the first degree, this relative ability is lost.* The person with an acute, undifferentiated or simple psychosis cannot maintain cerebral dominance or hemispheric integration unless he or she receives continuous cues and commands. Duhl (1978) tells a clinical anecdote about the problem of linear steps and the need for cueing. He had an autistic girl living in his home who was thoroughly acquainted with the household. If he asked her to bring an object to him, she could not find her way unless he vocally cued her at each turn in the journey. If he did not, she would become very disturbed and sometimes psychotic.

With the loss of cerebral dominance or hemispheric integration, there is a marked diminution of cortico-limbic modulation. The overall results appear in performance which requires an ability to separate items and sets, in a detectable disturbance in special electroencephalographic recordings, and in the clinical syndrome of disturbance of linearity and context. The psychotic in this stage is circumstantial, distractible, panicky and unable to carry out simple life assignments.

We can conjecture that the neural subsystems come into a state of cyclic loops. The corebrain, in an unmodulated state, fails to temper reticular control of attention, and there is no way to reduce sensory inputs (except possibly by flight). The cerebral cortex is flooded by afferent impulses from the sensory tracts and from the visceral afferents of the corebrain and the body. It is unable to mount linear cortical processes and balanced interhemispheric loops, so the problem in modulating corebrain states and sensory inputs is sustained or increased.

An unstable equilibrium has certain inevitable results. It can be stabilized by feedback or cybernetic controls from processes at another level (someone can reestablish a sustaining relationship with the acute psychotic person). Or the instability can be sustained (the acute psychosis becomes chronic), or a runaway occurs, a positive feedback or amplification of dysfunction (the psychosis gets worse and proceeds to a further degree).

The Second or Paranoid Order of Psychosis

Some psychotic episodes show a progression to a second order of disturbance. In this order of disturbance the patient imagines that the actions of other people are directed toward him. He has hallucinations which are usually auditory in schizophrenia. He may show more of a penchant for fight than flight, and he may even show a restitutive ability at linear cognition and ordered behavior in a focus upon dealing with his enemies.

In this degree of psychosis, we have indications of a special instance of sensory activity. The paranoid schizophrenic projects or "broadcasts" sensory images. Images which are ordinarily conceived of as thoughts are now believed to be occurring outside the body. In psychological interpretations we conclude that the patient is imagining voices or external events, but in neural terms we must consider another explanation. There are neural subsystems which consist of pathways from the sensory cortex to the sensory nuclei of the brainstem and to the bipolar cells of the retina. It may be that corticofugal impulses are actually transmitted to the sensory way stations (Pribram 1971). If so, there is a reversal of the usual polarity of sensory impulses. There is more to this story, however. On other grounds we must consider that the paranoid type of psychosis is not simply a degree of psychotic disorganization. I will come back later to the special case of schizophrenia of the paranoid type.

The Third Order of Psychosis

In clinical terms, some acute undifferentiated types of psychosis do not ameliorate. They are sustained and become "chronic." There are, however, some differences. While the acutely psychotic patient may desperately seek some form of social restitution or contact, the chronically psychotic patient may resist all attempts at engagement and become markedly withdrawn, becoming paranoid or combative at attempts to invade his privacy. He may take on silly facial expressions and mannerisms or establish relationships to objects or imaginary people. In this case, we say the patient is hebephrenic.

The engagement with fantasy and imagery is so marked in this state of psychosis that we might postulate that the center of cortical activity has shifted to the posterior cortex. There is a sensory cortex and corebrain dominance, so to speak. The disorganization of the more anterior lobes remains manifest in this degree of psychosis.

Psychosis of the Fourth Order

Sometimes the psychosis progresses rapidly to a serious loss of consciousness. The patient seems to be in a dream state. He refuses nourishment and contact with a desperate fanaticism; left alone, he will race about frantically or lie immobile in a stupor. At most, the face shows an occasional flash of panic or amusement, but even the face may freeze into a mask of immobility. The body is rigid, but one part of it may show a rocking or oscillatory movement, as in third order psychosis.

We conjecture now that the patient has lost all cerebral organization. The behavior and organismic state remind us very much of the REM or "D" states of sleep. We can conjecture that the psychotic patient is indeed in such a state and that the focus of neural activity has passed as far dorsally as the brainstem or pons (Hobson and McCarley, 1977).

The Special Case of Paranoid Schizophrenia

Some psychotic people seem to pass through a paranoid phase on their way to a chronic undifferentiated or hebephrenic picture. Others have paranoid elements or paranoid phases during psychotic episodes of other orders, although this is by no means always the case. Some paranoid psychotics have been paranoid before they were deemed psychotic. In fact, many have had a life history of hyper-independent, isolated, belligerent and antisocial behavior. In addition, many of the people we diagnose as paranoid schizophrenics have a remarkable ability at linear order and an almost uncanny sense of context. Consequently, we can argue that paranoid schizophrenia is not just a degrees of psychotic disorganization. We can say it is often a distinctly different type of schizophrenia. Some have argued that this behavioral configuration is not even schizophrenia.

There are grounds other than clinical observation for this argument. Gur (1978) has produced experimental evidence that the temporal cortex is overactive in schizophrenic psychosis of the paranoid type. There is also evidence of high levels of norepinephrine in this area in paranoid schizophrenia (see Chapter 9). The idea of an overactive temporal lobe also accords with our neurological experience. For example, electrical stimulation of the temporal lobe during surgery results in hallucinatory images (Penfield, 1969). Furthermore, tumors of the temporal lobe often produce delusions and hallucinations. (This matter will concern us again in Chapter 9.)

SUMMARY

We can describe the dysfunction in non-psychotic degrees of schizophrenia in a number of disciplinary languages. In psychological approaches we can see it as a deficiency in ego strength or cognitive structure. In behavioral terms, we can depict it as a problem in maintaining linear order and relating act or thought to event and context. In neurophysiological language, we can say it is a problem in cerebral organization and temporo-limbic-corebrain modulation. A deficit in TLC, so to speak.

A variety of factors may enable the schizophrenic person to maintain a tenuous state of non-psychotic adjustment. Among these is a social dependency and a dependency upon a field of cues. When this contact is lost, the schizophrenic person suffers a further loss of cerebral organization which we term psychosis.

9

The Neurosynaptic Fields

in Schizophrenia

In Chapter 8, I reviewed evidence that schizophrenia involves a problem in the integration of cortical and intercerebral connections. There is more to say about this. On the one hand, I have not yet taken up the important cortico-limbic and corebrain systems; on the other hand, a question arises: Can we pin down the schizophrenic problem any more closely?

In one sense of the word we can. We can allocate it to the structure of the grey sheets of the cortex and the grey columns of the corebrain and the limbic system. This identification will take us to an examination of the structure of grey matter and to issues of how the grey matter forms in the process of maturation.

The surmise that a deficiency in the development of grey matter exists in schizophrenia leads us to an important consideration that we have already postponed too long. Such a deficiency is but one context of schizophrenia and psychotic disorganization. There are, as well, psychological loops in the process and a social context. I will therefore close this chapter with a comment about the need for a broader paradigm and the development of a neuropsychology with social perspectives.

In Chapter 8 our conclusion was this: In schizophrenia there seems to be a problem in the integration of all cortical and interhemispheric function. In our classical paradigms we have been uncomfortable with such general statements, and we have tried to pin down more precise locations or sources of problems. Therefore, perhaps we should ask if the schizophrenic disorder can be further localized in the nervous system.

THE TEMPORO-LIMBIC-COREBRAIN PATHWAYS AND THE EMOTIONAL PROBLEM OF SCHIZOPHRENIA

Before we can narrow our perspective, we must temporarily broaden it, for we have said too little about a system of connections which often has been given a central role in the schizophrenic problem.

The lateral surface of the temporal lobe receives sensory impulses of hearing and plays a part in the integration of cortical functions, for it has association tracts to all other cortical areas, but the rest of the temporal lobe is an important way station in another pathway too. It receives fibers from the frontal poles and sends fibers to a very ancient subsystem of the brain. This subsystem is called the "limbic system"; it used to be called the "seat of the emotions," but it is only one subsystem in the activities which are termed "emotional" in clinical circles (see Chapter 5).

This ancient system has a cortex which lies around the corpus collosum in the space between the hemispheres and along the inner surface of each cerebral hemisphere. This cortex is directly connected to the temporal lobe and sends fibers to basal ganglia and to the core-brain. To be more accurate, the limbic cortex projects fibers in three principal pathways. It projects to the caudate nucleus and amygdala of the extrapyramidal system; it also projects in a loop under the corpus callosum to the mammillary bodies and thence to the lateral portions of the hypothalamus and probably from there to the reticular activating system (more on this later).

Pribram (1971) interrupted the limbic system of monkeys by removing both amydaloid nuclei. There were no gross disturbances in the behavior of these monkeys after the surgery, but each one in turn lost his position in the dominance hierarchy of the colony. In some subtle way the aggressivity of the dominant position was lost. Taussig (cited by Pribram, 1971) studied a man who had suffered the removal of both limbic lobes in surgery. This man was capable of doing linear tasks which he had long known but he could not remember new ones. One day he was told that the laboratory would be closed on the following Thursday for Thanksgiving. On Thanksgiving Day the man got dressed and went to the lab anyway even though he said to himself that he should not bother since the lab was closed. Apparently, then, the limbic system is critical in connecting the task and the vocal command or cue. Taussig's patient knew how to dress and get to the lab and he remembered the command not to go, but he could not connect the two.

Pribram (1971) reports the case of a very obese woman with bilateral limbic destruction. She reported that she was not hungry, but when food was served, she surged into the room, knocked others aside and ravenously stuffed her mouth with both hands.

These cases suggest that a marked disorder of vegetative functions occurs with a limbic order interruption; in addition, behavior does not accord with ideation. Presumably, the woman with limbic lesions had no way to order herself to desist from gluttony. Collectively, these cases indicate that the rostral portion of the limbic system is important in integrating motor behaviors with a knowledge of when and where such behaviors are to be carried out. In other words, the limbic system is also important in the relation of act and context. The more posterior portions of the limbic system are believed to allow the cortex to inhibit the corebrain and the reticular activating system. In psychological terms, this route allows an inhibition of emotionality when concentrating upon a task (maintaining cerebral dominance). In the psychoanalytic metaphor, the limbic system is the pathway by which the ego suppresses or controls the id.

These surgical findings about the limbic system bear a faint resemblance to the vegetative and emotional disturbances of schizophrenia, but by no means do they lead us to assume a schizophrenic disorder. In short, we cannot equate schizophrenia with a disturbance in the limbic system alone. It appears instead that the corebrain (and emotional) disturbances in schizophrenia and its psychoses may be incident to a lack of limbic modulation, but they are disturbances of the corebrain and not of the limbic pathways in and of themselves.

THE CENTRALITY OF THE TEMPORAL LOBE

In Chapter 8, it was pointed out that the temporal lobe plays a vital role in the pathways of cerebral integration and motor completion. I have also pointed out some evidence that the temporal lobe is instrumental in the projection of sensory experience in the paranoid states of schizophrenic psychosis. Now it appears that the temporal lobe is important in the limbic-corebrain connections, for those pathways begin in the medial and underside of this region of the cerebrum. In sum, the temporal lobe is the anatomic origin for some pathways to the motor area, for pathways to the sensory nuclei and for the limbic to corebrain projections. On this account, the temporal lobe seems to play a central role in neural organization of the cerebrum.

Each of the pathways which arise in the temporal lobe are in fact feedback loops which return fibers to the temporal lobe as well. These include the fronto-temporo-motor pathway which has return fibers from the basal ganglia and from the muscle bundles; the cortico-sensory tracts which return thalamo-cortical fibers and the limbic system, which also returns fibers to the temporal cortex. Thus, we can say that the temporal lobe is an important link in all three of these major circuits.

For this reason it pays us to ask if there is evidence of a temporal lobe disorder in schizophrenia. In the case of paranoid psychosis there is little question that this is so. I have mentioned this in previous chapters, and it will concern us again. In addition, it has been shown by Flor (1969) that among patients with a brain tumor of the left temporal lobe, 90 percent have auditory hallucinations and delusions. So it is rather clear that paranoid schizophrenic patients have a manifest temporal lobe disorder. However, we cannot make this assertion about schizophrenia without psychosis or about other psychotic states in schizophrenia. At best we could argue that the deficit in linearity and corebrain modulation suggests the pos-

sibility, but the cerebral dysfunctions of schizophrenia do not originate in the temporal lobe, nor are they confined to it.

In short, the temporal lobe is a critical node in the processes of
schizophrenia, but we cannot localize schizophrenia as a disorder of
temporal lobe activity.

SCHIZOPHRENIA AS A DISORDER OF GREY
MATTER FIELDS

We cannot come up with a good old-time Aristotelian solution
and claim we have found the focal lesion and the source of schizophrenia, but we can make a more specific statement. Schizophrenia
is not a disorder of long fiber tracts. It is not a response to a stimulus;
it does not lie in some associational pathway. In fact, it reflects a widespread cortical and corebrain dysfunction, and it arises in those very
areas of the brain which generate images, plans and activities. Therefore, schizophrenia is a disorder of grey matter and its integration. It
is a disorder of cortical fields and subcortical grey columns. So we
must turn our attention to the structure of these grey fields.

On the Structure of Grey Fields

In our anatomy books we will find maps of over 40 areas of the
grey cortex of the cerebrum, and in the brainstem there are hundreds
of separate nuclei which are distinguished by appearance and cellular
form. But we must not assume on this account that the brain operates
as a discrete series of nuclear actions. In terms of activity, these
myriad divisions function collectively. The cortex of the entire cerebrum can function as a single sheet of grey matter, and the many
nuclei of the corebrain can be activated as continuous columns of
grey matter, from the hypothalamus to the spinal cord.

We can conceive of the cortical mantle and the cerebral grey
column as fields. They do not depend solely on sensory input for
their activity. They generate their own electrical wave activity and
have their own metabolism. Within these fields, cells can multiply,
grow and cluster.

In the presystems days of neurophysiology, we looked for the main
elements of the grey matter and hence made a series of reductive

selections like we did in any old-fashioned science. Of the two main sorts of brain cells, the neurones and the glial cells, we paid selective attention to the neurones. We attributed to the glial cells a purely supportive role in the nervous system. Of the various types of neurones, we concentrated on the largest ones with the long axones which gave rise to the white tracts. We tended then to ignore the small neurones with short axones which were found in the grey matter. Of the processes of the neurone, we paid more attention to the axones than to the dendrites. We got so absorbed in the study of the individual neurone and its electrical conductivity that we almost ignored the tiny spaces (or synapses) by which neuronal networks are enjoined.

With the neuroscience revolution, there has been a shift in this view of the neural fields. We suspect now that the glial cells have a critical function in the storage of images or memory, and that this storage is referenced and retrievable by systems involving millions of short and long axoned neurones (Pribram, 1971). We observe that the dendrites branch so richly that the dendritic processes of a single neurone may connect with hundreds of thousands of other neurones. At each of these connections is a synapse. Conductivity across these synapses requires a complex biochemical process mediated by substances called neurotransmitters.

Since the neural subsystems of the cerebrum are connected by sheets and columns of grey matter, there must be a problem in schizophrenia in these neural fields. In fact, there is mounting evidence of a problem in neurosynaptic transmission in the neural fields of certain brain areas at least in the psychotic stages of schizophrenia. I shall now briefly review some of this evidence and the location of the difficulty.

The Disturbance of Catecholamines

There is considerable evidence that a disturbance in neurotransmission disrupts the neural fields in schizophrenia. We must briefly review this evidence and try to assess its significance.*

---

* I have had personal experience with clinical and research approaches to all of the other levels of schizophrenia covered in this volume, but I have had no experience with the cellular and molecular levels which are discussed in this chapter. For this reason, I have had to rely on books and papers for my information. If my statements are sophomoric, I hope they will not be used to discredit the main thrust of the thesis.

Two catecholamines, dopamine and norepinephrine, are critical in the corebrain and in parts of the cerebrum for the transmission of impulses across the neurosynaptic junction. There are two sorts of evidence of a disturbance in both of these catecholamines in the brains of schizophrenic people. The first is the finding of increased levels of these substances in the brains of schizophrenic people at postmortem examination. Increased levels of norepinephrine have been reported in the temporal lobe and in the corebrain (Farley et al., 1978). Increased levels of dopamine have been reported in the septal area, the nucleus ambiguens, and other portions of the limbic system (Bird, 1978; Crow and Owen, 1978).

The other line of evidence is psychopharmacological. *Disturbances in the level of dopamine are found in the very areas of the brain at which the antipsychotic action of the phenothiazines is believed to occur.* The simplest account of this concurrence has been offered by Carlsson (1978), who reports a disturbance in dopamine levels in the limbic system, the substantia nigra and the infundibulum. The antipsychotic action of phenothiazines is believed to be exerted upon the limbic system. The extrapyramidal effects are believed to be upon the substantia nigra, and certain metabolic disturbances such as hirsutism, which occurs with prolonged administration of pheno-thiazines, are generally located in the infundibular pathways. The theory, then, is that dopamine transmission is disordered in the very areas of phenothiazine action and that phenothiazines probably replace dopaminergic effects at the level of synaptic transmission.

There is probably much more complexity to this problem of neuro-transmission than Carlsson's account would suggest. In the first place, it may not be that a deviation in levels of dopamines is an issue in vivo. Instead, there may be a disorder of the dopamine receptors in the post-synaptic neuronal junction. In addition, disturbances in dopamine levels are found more extensively in the basal ganglia and the limbic system than is indicated in Carlsson's review (1978). The disorders are not limited to dopamine, for norepinephrine levels in the limbic system, the basal gaglia and the temporal lobe are also found (Farley et al., 1978).

The evidence of some disturbance in the metabolism of catechol-amines is considerable, but at this point the significance of these findings is far from clear. It is not clear what the disturbances are in the living brain. We cannot say whether there is a mean increase in both catecholamine levels or whether some disturbance exists in the balance of dopamine and norepinephrine. So far, the finding of an increase in norepinephrine in paranoid psychosis seems relatively clear, but we do not have clear information about whether dopamine levels are related to the degree or type of psychosis.

To make matters more confusing, it is difficult to interpret these findings at more clinical levels. Should we expect a decrease in receptivity to dopamine to equal an increase in dopamine level by some mechanism of compensation? Would an increase in dopamine in the limbic system indicate increased limbic and extrapyramidal activity in the living state? If so, would this be apparent on clinical grounds? Would it account for the hyperemotionality or the increased muscular tonus of many schizophrenic states?

If there is simply an increased level of dopamine in the limbic and basal ganglia, and if this is associated with a hyperactivity of these brain areas, it is quite logical to speculate that this hyperactivity is associated with increased muscle tonus, the mood disturbances and the vegetative disorders of schizophrenia. However, if increased catecholamine levels are incident to a decreased receptivity or if receptivity is in fact decreased, such speculations would not find support in the data. I doubt if we can answer these issues until we can correlate levels of catecholamines to the form and state of the psychosis.

The finding of a transmissional problem in the corebrain brings up another major question. Are these findings related to the schizophrenic problem in cerebral organization, or are they, in fact, a second and unrelated finding?* It is more interesting to assume a

---

* There are three other less supported theories of the molecular dysfunctions in schizophrenia. These are: 1) an orthomolecular view which is based upon the assumption of certain similarities between schizophrenia and the psychosis of pellagra; 2) a transmethylization hypothesis which is based upon the similarities of paranoid psychosis to reactions to drugs such as mescaline; and 3) a hypothesis that B-endorphin secretion is abnormal in schizophrenia.

I will not consider these hypotheses here. The first two are generally discredited because there is no evidence of their occurrence and because the analogies are unacceptable. The B-endorphin hypothesis is not discredited, but I shall regard it as too new for inclusion in this text.

relationship, and we can do this by making a highly speculative theory.

Neural Field Activity and Degrees of Psychosis

Suppose we consider two generalizations which may prove much too simplistic but can serve to initiate our sequence of postulates. First of all, dopamine activity seems to be aberrant in the limbic system in schizophrenic psychosis since its action is apparently replaced by phenothiazines. This idea at the level of synaptic fields correlates with the grosser finding that the forebrain cortex fails to modulate the corebrain in the psychotic states of schizophrenia. The other generalization in this: In the paranoid, overactive states of schizophrenia, there seems to be an increase in norepinephrine in the temporal lobe and the reticular activating system, which occurs with a general overactivity of temporal cortical activity.

On these bases we can spin a theory. Let's assume that there is no evident disorder of neurotransmission in schizophrenia in the non-psychotic states. But it is probable, on grounds I will state later, that there is a relative deficiency of dopamine. Suppose we call it a latent or potential deficiency which is part of a general underdevelopment of the neurosynaptic fields, at least in the fronto-temporal-limbic fields and pathways. With the onset of psychosis, the dopaminergic activity of this system is inadequate to deal with the stress of continual attempts at inhibition of the corebrain. Thus, the syndrome of the psychotic onset features a loss of linear abilities and cerebral dominance, a loss of corebrain modulation and an exhaustion of dopaminergic activity.

In this circumstance the lateral temporal lobe, too, is released from fronto-temporal-parietal inhibition. In neurophysiological terms, it is no longer possible to maintain cerebral dominance. The lateral temporal cortex becomes "overactive" and may actually develop an excess of norepinephrine. In this situation, the situation of hyperactive and paranoid psychosis, the temporal lobe becomes a relatively autonomous center of cortical activity. It can then issue cortico-sensory impulses which "broadcast" cortical images to peripheral centers as hallucinations and the other perceptual distortions so

characteristic in the psychosis. But temporal and corebrain hyperactivity is exhaustible. In a few days or weeks, the signs of temporal
hyperactivity may lessen and so may the acute emotionality of corebrain overactivity. The psychotic person may become generally
disoriented, confused, unable to remember, more quiet and withdrawn. The stage we call chronic psychosis has been reached with a
third stage of cerebral disorganization. Or sometimes the second stage
manifestations become more quiescent, but a chronic paranoid psychosis with occasional flare-ups continues. More hopefully, the process
of psychotic disorganization is halted by antipsychotic drugs, social
reaffiliation or other means, and the cerebral disorganization is
reversed.

As I said in Chapter 5, I think there are still further stages of
cerebral disorganization in which centers of relatively automatic
activity shift caudally to the brainstem. In the normal dream or REM
states of sleep, there is extensive inhibition of sensory inputs, extrapyramidal mechanisms for tonicity and cerebral activities. In this
organismic state, spontaneous impulses arise from large neurones in
the dorsal portion of the pons and transmit waves of activity to the
oculo-motor nuclei in the brainstem and to the cerebral cortex (Hobson and McCarley, 1977). In some of the deepest, most disorganized
stages of psychosis, a similar state seems to exist. One observable
feature is the constant, oscillating movement of some body part,
indicating a center of autonomous neural activity in the basal ganglia.

If we ask how widespread is the neurosynaptic disturbance in
schizophrenia, we will have to make a distinction before we can
answer. In the psychotic states of schizophrenia, the functional
disturbance can be so complete that the entire central nervous system
is involved. Aside from speculations, we can say at this point only that
some disturbance of grey neuronal fields seems to exist in schizophrenia. It may be a disturbance in neurosynaptic transmission or a
broader disturbance in dendritic connections (see below). It appears
to affect the cerebral cortex in general or at least the temporo-limbic
and corebrain axis.

Whatever the nature of this neurosynaptic dysfunction proves to
be, we are not warranted in jumping to the conclusion about it which
was traditional in the biological paradigm. We cannot conclude that

a disease or even a genetic disorder in metabolism is *necessarily* the cause of the difficulty, for there is an alternative possibility. This we will uncover as we examine the development of the neuronal fields in the course of postnatal development.

THE DEVELOPMENT OF THE NEUROSYNAPTIC FIELDS

There is an important aspect of the cortical grey structure that we have so far ignored. We have said nothing about the development of these fields in childhood, and this is a critical matter in our understanding of schizophrenia.

The Classical Problem of Neuronal Number

In past decades we could see no evidence of development or learning in the cerebrum. The adult number of cortical axones was present at birth and no increase in these neurones or in the axones of the white matter accompanied the process of human development. So there was no neuroanatomical or neurophysiological change which accompanied human development. Learning, then, was regarded vaguely as a "functional" change to be explained by psychological theories alone.

It should also be noted too that many investigators had counted the number of cortical neurones per square millimeter in cases of chronic schizophrenia. No decrease could be shown. So we also had no evidence of a perceptible problem in the neurosynaptic fields in schizophrenia. Such negative findings confirmed the old notion that we should distinguish between "organic" and "functional" disorders of the nervous system. Disorders with detachable lesions became the province of neurology, while the latter were relegated to the psychologies. The rift between the two sciences gradually increased in the psychoanalytic era, and we had no way to put the contributions of these disciplines together.

Neurosynaptic and Glial Proliferation

We had looked in the wrong place. There is no neuronal proliferation with development in childhood, but *there is a massive prolifera-*

tion of the dendritic processes of the neurone (Pribram, 1971). Since each dendritic branch forms a synaptic connection with an axone of another neurone, *there is thus a great increase in the number of neurosynaptic junctions.* In short, postnatal development is accompanied by a geometric increase in the number of neural connections and hence in the complexity of the grey matter.

Such an increase in the number of synaptic connections must be accompanied by an increase in the metabolism of neurotransmitters such as dopamine and norepinephrine, for the synapse requires such substances for neurotransmission. We can conjecture, then, that the metabolism of neurotransmitters and the proliferation of dendrites must occur together in postnatal life, for one enables the other. This interdependence of development between neurotransmitters and dendritic branches can lead us to several hypothetical assumptions, though at present we lack direct evidence of their occurrence. It seems probable that any prenatal failure in the metabolism of neurotransmitters could result in a failure of dendritic proliferation. But analogously we must argue that any postnatal failure in dendritic proliferation could result in a deficiency of neurosynaptic metabolism.

There is more to the developmental picture of the grey matter fields. Since the microstructure is a system of elements, all of its elements proliferate together. As each dendritic process subdivides, a glial cell next to it also divides by mitosis (Pribram, 1971). The new dendritic branch then lies between two glial cells. Then, as the dendrite branches again, each of these glial cells also splits to form two more, and so on. The result is a pattern of dendritic branches, each of which is flanked by glial cells in an intimate anatomic arrangement. The proliferation of dendrites and glial cells occurs together, and these occur with the development of the neurosynaptic junctions and their neuroendocrinological mediation.

The demonstration of a developmental relationship between dendritic and glial proliferation allows us a hypothesis about memory or information storage. Many investigators now believe that the glial cells act as "addresses" for the storage of information, probably on the macromolecules of the glial cells (Pribram, 1971). The dendrites are then viewed as the routes of access or retrieval for this information, somewhat in the manner of the electronic computer. If this is the case, the dendritic-glial proliferation in human development constitutes the anatomic substrate for the growth of memory and experience.

In short, the elements of the neurosynaptic or grey fields of the nervous system *develop together* as in any system at any level of organization. The spinal nerves and the musculature develop together or not at all, for instance. The central nervous system, the neuromuscular abilities and the life experience of the organism evolve together too. From a systems perspective we do not regard the development of one element of a system as the cause of the development of the others; instead, each is interdependent.

The Significance of These Findings

The developmental interdependence of these elements of the neurosynaptic field does not allow us to continue old dichotomies between functional and organic. We no longer have to imagine that development is associated with some unseen change in the relationship between neurones in the cortex. We have instead a quite visible neuroanatomy of the microstructure, and we can postulate a neurophysiology which is beginning to become known. By the same token, we cannot allow a dichotomy between theories of development at this level being either genetic *or* acquired. As I suggested above, a genetic inadequacy of neurometabolism could result in a failure of synaptic proliferation, but, in turn, such a failure of any kind would not be likely to stimulate a postnatal development of metabolism.

We can make this point at the organismic level in respect to the development of schizophrenia. The postnatal development of the human infant's nervous system does not occur apart from experience, and *human interaction is a critical dimension of this experience*. The human infant does not even sit up, walk or speak unless it has interpersonal experience (Spitz, 1946). Therefore, we can insist that voice, touch, gaze and other early interactional experiences must be critical in organizing the nervous system and developing the microstructure of the cortex. Later, of course, the acquisition of speech or psychomotor skills and then of a measure of cerebral dominance must be important too. But *muscular-environmental contact in general, and human interaction in particular, are the first organismic experiences.*

Consider the assertion once more, and then we shall see what we can make of it in regard to schizophrenia. I am saying that there is an interdependence in human development of events at the social, organismic and suborganismic levels. Interaction at the social level, neurobehavioral skill at the organismic level, neural organization in organ systems, dendritic-synaptic-glial proliferation at the cellular level, and catecholamine metabolism at the metabolic level are interdependent processes. One does not occur without the other.

On this basis, we can make postulates about the earliest loops in the development of schizophrenia:

1) It could be that a genetic or other prenatal disorder impairs the metabolism or mitotic potential of the microstructure so that the infant cannot utilize or participate in postnatal experience, as many genetic theorists now hold; or

2) a failure in postnatal, interactional experience could result in a failure of neuro-synaptic development, as I conjectured in Chapter 4.

Any combination or intermediate possibility could exist too, and we must not make our theories dichotomous. It could be, for example, that a genetically deficient infant requires special and forceful interactional contacts to prevent schizophrenia. Possibly, a relatively inert infant with a low level of neurometabolism falls behind in neuro-synaptic development if there is a relatively deficient interactional experience in the early days and weeks of postnatal life. In short, the prenatal and postnatal problems may feed on each other to escalate a deficiency in development at all levels. In cybernetic terms, any deficiency in this process can be subject to amplification, for the less attentive infant is least likely to gain an adequate interactional experience, and the child thus deficient is less able to accomplish later stages of learning.

If these conjectures be so, we should be able to find a relative insufficiency of dendritic branching and glial cells in at least the temporal cortex and the temporo-limbic systems. Possibly such deficiencies are much more widespread in the grey matter of schizophrenic people. But in any event, a deficiency in dendritic-glial proliferation is the visible and neuroanatomic equivalent to a neuropharmacological finding of a catecholamine disorder.

This notion of complementarity between genetic and experiential processes is borne out by the two findings about the role of genetic histories in schizophrenia. It is abundantly clear that genetic background plays a role in at least some cases of schizophrenia (Kety et al., 1971). It is equally clear that schizophrenia cannot be explained on genetic grounds alone.

I am still concerned that we might consider the catecholamine dysfunction or the problem of cerebral organization out of context and view one of them as *the* schizophrenic problem or as the cause of schizophrenia. For this reason, I will quickly review some of the broader contexts of these schizophrenic problems.

At the suborganismic level, it may be that the dopamine and norepinephrine problems themselves are incident to a breakdown of cerebral organization in the states of psychosis. But, as I have just argued, these neurotransmissional difficulties are also part and parcel of the general development of the neuronal fields of the nervous system and therefore have a psychological and social context, i.e., they are dependent in part upon the development of the human infant.

There are also psychological contexts for the later developments of the schizophrenic problem. For one thing, the social and task failures of the schizophrenic child engender a sense of failure and inadequacy which can lead to a further avoidance of experience and a social withdrawal. This in turn can further interfere with the organization of cerebral dominance and the ability to achieve it. For this reason, no neurophysiological finding in the future study of schizophrenia will obviate the need for a psychology of schizophrenia (see Summary). Pribram (1971) has devoted his career to the evolution of a "neuropsychology." At the least, one must argue that no one needs psychotherapy and coaching as much as the child who is falling into a failure of the maturational process, no matter what the reasons for the failure. Insofar as our present methods of education and psychotherapy do not have adequate measures for preventing such maturational failures, we must develop methods which do.

In addition, the ability to effect and maintain cerebral dominance for short periods of time is in part a matter of volition. To varying degrees people can minimize distractibility and sit down to write a letter or figure income tax when it is time to do so. In some measure the ability is also a function of the situation. We may need a desk, a set of papers, a quiet room and a propitious time of the day or week in order to accomplish the set task. The borderline person needs an even more structured situation for linear accomplishments. Often this consists of at least a familiar physical field of props and cues and the presence of an authoritarian other who can provide verbal instructions or cues, or act as a safeguard against distractions. In fact, the very prevention of a psychotic break may depend upon a stable field of physical cues and the proximity of a symbiotic partner. I have already cited the case of Charlie who became openly psychotic upon the discovery that his bedroom walls had been stripped of photographs of faces and eyes. I consider this a common experience. Divorces, deaths, leaving for college or military service are common events in the precipitation of psychosis, and in part these separations also involve the leaving of familiar places. I recently saw a young man who developed hallucinations when he was away from a symbolic eye which his father had placed on his bedroom wall to prevent him from masturbating.

Jaynes (1976) has pointed out the relation of hallucinations to separation from authoritarian figures in ancient people with "bicameral" minds. He pointed out that when people had lost their superiors, they tried to preserve their faces or gazes in symbolic form and so hallucinated their commands and instructions.

In short, it is possible that psychological and social events form contexts for microevents as small as the processes of neurotransmission. Such contexts certainly play a role in the ability to maintain cerebral dominance or cerebral organization. On the other hand, we must not lean from one extreme to the other in our understanding of causation. Events at various levels maintain and influence each other. It is not conceivable that the schizophrenic dysfunction in catecholamines is simply a failure to sustain social contexts of a supportive nature, for all people experience such failures. In short, we are not likely to find any one level of causation for schizophrenia any more than we are for tuberculosis. An infection with the tubercle bacillus is a necessary but insufficient cause for clinical tuberculosis, which has as well a systemic and a demographical level of causation.

Because of the importance of this way of thinking systemically about the schizophrenic problem, I have added a summary to this volume which reviews the multiple levels of dysfunction and speculates upon how a deviation such as schizophrenia can evolve and escalate.

10

Summary: The Nature and Development of Schizophrenia

Lewis Carroll's Queen of Hearts might have said that schizophrenia means anything I want it to mean, and this is how it was in the old epistemology of science. The adherents of each doctrine would choose one factor from a long list and make that one the essence and cause of schizophrenia. But we are in a new era of science. Schizophrenia is all of the factors and loops of its nature—and more. It is the totality of these. Yet to have an ordered picture of this wholeness, we must do more than list the elements or views. We must have a comprehensible way of clustering them, and we must show how they are interrelated in the development of an instance.

LEVELS OF SCHIZOPHRENIA

The scheme I have used is borrowed from the general systems concepts of levels of organization. To use this, I have successively taken a perspective at eight levels of organization* from the societal

---

* A total of eight levels were covered, although this does not correspond to the number of chapters in the book. There were two chapters at the organismic level and Chapter 7 was devoted to the changing views of neuroscience.

to the molecular. I have tried to give a brief picture of schizophrenic dysfunction at each of these levels. I can summarize what I have said at each level as follows:

Level I. At the level of *societal organization*, madness is a deviance most consistently manifest by strange, sometimes violent, behavior which indicates a change in social identity. Other phenomena such as hallucinations may or may not be considered madness, depending upon the era or the culture. Schizophrenia, as the term is employed in America, is a concept of deficiency in autonomy and linear ability, according to the present standards of an industrial Western country.

Level II. Although psychosis and schizophrenia are defined by the norms of the society in general, the control and maintenance of these deviations is the province of the *institutions* of the society. Some institutions of medicine, psychiatry and law are in the business of controlling psychotic people. Unfortunately, the very measures which reduce psychosis can maintain schizophrenia. The concept of schizophrenia is also socially useful and legally convenient; the fear of psychosis can help maintain the existing social order. So some of our institutions are in the business of preserving, molding and handing down a lore of schizophrenia.

Level III. The *family* provides an environment, a communicational field, in which schizophrenia can develop. The decreasing size and strength of the Western family over the centuries have provided a deficient social environment which probably fosters symbiotic over-dependency between the surviving members. The symbiotic dependency so common in schizophrenia may also be a familial response to a subtly incompetent child, but the symbiosis also tends to split the family into opposing factors. In this situation a field of conflicting or "double-binding" instructions is provided for the growing child, and a schizophrenic mode of cognition and explanation is provided for the child's behavior.

Level IV. At the level of *dyadic relationships*, there is a tendency to cling to a confirming, supportive relationship. If this fails, the child may reject relationships altogether and fall into an autistic social existence. If we examine the behavior in such dyads, we notice a strong affiliation and mutual overdependency, but the partners do not turn to each other much for face-to-face interaction. When they do, there are significant deviations in interactional ability. These deviant interactional patterns characteristically appear between the schizophrenic family member and the mother, or it can be that another nurturing figure is part of the dyad instead of the mother. The mother, or other parental figure, does not always share the deviance and show it in other relationships. This deficiency in interaction between mother and child may be present from the earliest weeks of the neonatal period. This is a highly important deficit, for a mastery of interactional participation is a necessary basis for the development of cognitive and psychomotor skills.

Level V. At a fifth level of analysis, we can watch the schizophrenic *person.* Our observations on this score have been greatly confounded by the use of disciplinary abstractions such as the symptom lingo of medicine or the metaphors of academic and psychoanalytic psychology. As a consequence, we lack descriptions of the behavior of the schizophrenic person. Our view of the schizophrenic person has been further obscured by our failure to distinguish schizophrenic and psychotic states and various degrees of schizophrenic disorganization. If we abstain from making inferences about the underlying pathology and stick to observing the behavior of the non-psychotic schizophrenic person, we find a deficiency that is characteristic of schizophrenia at this level. There is a relative inability to complete complex linear sequences without cues or commands. There is a problem in relating actions to contexts, and there is a problem in modulating emotionality or corebrain functions.

Level VI. These schizophrenic problems in accomplishment seem to represent problems of the *nervous system.* They are not accompanied by disorders in the sensory tracts nor in the motor and neuromuscular system, so they must be localized in the cerebrum, especially in the forebrain. In past decades we have tried to describe this forebrain problem with the metaphors of psychology, e.g., as a cognitive deficiency or an ego weakness. But now we have learned enough about the neurophysiology of central processes that we can begin to describe the schizophrenic problem at this level in direct neural terms. In such terms, the schizophrenic person has a disorder a) in hemispheric integration, and b) in the functioning of the fronto-temporal-limbic system. In the psychotic phases of schizophrenia, there is a further breakdown in neural integration.

Levels VII and VIII. The neural systems involved are not made up solely of white tracts. They include continuous fields of grey matter which are "alive" or active in their own right. These fields consist of neuronal and glial cells which are joined by countless synapses. Transmission across these synapses is mediated by substances called neurotransmitters. In schizophrenia there is evidence of a disorder in the metabolism or utilization of two neurotransmitters, dopamine and norepinephrine. These are the neurotransmitters of the very areas which seem to be the site of the neural disorganization in schizophrenia and early psychosis.

The cortical neuronal fields develop with learning and experience. This development may depend upon early interactional contact. Infants who do not experience such contact do not even learn to sit up or speak. The development of neuronal fields does not consist of proliferation of new neurones. What proliferates are the dendritic branches of the neuron, the glial cells and the number of synapses. With a proliferation in synapses, an increased metabolism of dopamine and norepinephrine must develop. The fact that neural fields develop in this way does not allow us to dichotomize between genetic and acquired deficiencies. A development which begins prenatally must be continued by interactional experience and then by solitary learning. At these levels schizophrenia seems to be a lack of development in the neuronal grey fields. The inadequate dendritic connections and neuroendocrine development may be prenatal and postnatal.

A CYBERNETIC INTEGRATION

To have a more integrated picture of schizophrenia we can describe the problem at each level and then try to say how each level of dysfunction is interrelated with the others. Cybernetics furnishes us with a mode. At any moment in time, processes cause and maintain each other.

Consider an example. At the level of the family, the mother-child symbiosis maintains a schism in the family. Opposition and detachment from others strengthen the symbiotic attachment between the mother and child. This attachment in turn deprives the child of time with third parties which could provide a learning experience. Certain skills do not develop, resulting in social failures for the growing child. The failures in turn lead the child back to over-dependency on the mother, which deprives the child of other experiences, tightens the symbiotic alliance, further alienates the father, and so on. We could carry out this depiction of vicious cycles at all levels until we had a picture of negative feedback loops and stasis from the social to the microstructural level.

The Amplification of Deviance

Negative feedback and vicious cycles are not static for an indefinite period of time. They tend to escalate. The clinic gets more and more clients, and there is less and less staff time for each one. The results are less propitious, and the old clients stay on. The cleavage in the family grows as each member finds other contacts or withdraws more and more. The hurt and angry schizophrenic child makes less effort to make connections and accomplish. But there is even more to the problem. As the child grows older, more and more is expected of him by family, then by school and neighborhood. *The deviance amplifies in accordance with an increasing set of demands.* Failures are more hurtful and result in increasing withdrawal and self-rejection. The escalation is not confined to a single level of dysfunction. The problem of the mother-child dyad becomes more and more a family problem. The problem of the family becomes a problem of the school and then of the neighborhood.

To account for rapid change in shorter durations we can make use of the cybernetic model of positive feedback. This term does not mean in cybernetics what it has come to mean humorously in clinical circles. A positive feedback is not a pleasant or friendly response to something one has just said. In cybernetics, a positive feedback is an effect which enhances its own cause to produce an escalation of change. If such an escalation is unchecked, it is often called a "runaway."

The psychosis is an example. Something like this may happen: This schizophrenic person, dependent upon cues for cognitive order, breaks from the partner and then experiences a disorganization of thought. This is accompanied by panic, so the psychotic person takes off and runs away from familiar surroundings. The cognitive disorganization gets worse and cortico-sensory activities produce a reversal of perceptual priorities, resulting in paranoid distortions. The psychotic person now attacks the objects of dependency and further escalates the alienation. An extreme overactivity of neural fields may cause a depletion of neurotransmitters, which results in a further measure of cerebral disorganization, until the ability to make social contact is virtually lost.

We can use the cybernetic model of positive feedback to explain a slow escalation of deviance and thus make up a likely story about the evolution of schizophrenia in childhood. Possibly an innate decrease in attentiveness in the newborn makes it difficult for the mother to form contact. Possibly the parents fail to even make an attempt. In either event, an early deficiency in communicational relationships results in a failure to learn interactional behavior and a failure to develop neuronal fields and cerebral dominance. This failure in turn makes later cognitive development difficult and encourages either parental rejection and autism or parental over-protection and symbiotic attachment. The second occurrence may in turn further limit the child's opportunity for social experience and make his learning conditional upon the parent's presence or aegis. Meanwhile, social failures and parental loyalties lead to a psychological defensiveness with traits such as grandiosity, withdrawal, disdain, social anxieties and other personality qualities which still further inhibit the maturational experience and strengthen the overdependency. Thus, the schizophrenia spirals as more and more is expected of the growing child.

The Relationship Between Levels

The adequacy of a process or function at any level is constrained or limited by the adequacy of its component processes at sublevels.

The adequacy of a society to avoid or treat psychosis is limited by the capacities and abilities of its institutions and its professions. The ability of the mother and child to interrelate is constrained by the reactivity of the child. But a failure in function at any level is also attended by a failure at intralevels, and this too is likely to escalate. The inadequate institution accumulates psychotic patients who become more and more incapacitated. The failure of the parent-child interaction may lead to the withdrawal of both participants.

This principle can be stated more affirmatively. A problem in dysfunction at any level of organization is ideally corrected at higher levels of organization. The failing institution should receive support and more adequate information from the society as a whole. The inadequate mother-infant relationship should be corrected by the family as a whole, and the inadequacy of neuronal field development should be improved by neural systems and interactional compensations.

When this compensation fails, when a dysfunction is not corrected at the next higher level of organization, still higher levels must be brought into play. If the neurosynaptic deficit is not correctable by the general level of neural activity and interaction, the problem becomes a problem which requires the attention of the larger family, then of the institutions concerned with development and then of the society as a whole. In this sense, every schizophrenic person is a statement of societal failure. But the declination is downward as well. Every schizophrenic person also reflects the failure of family, of neural organization and of metabolic activity. At the least, a failure of the corrective possibilities insures a frozen status of inadequate development. At the worst, this failure leads to a steady decline at every level of organization. Most of the seriously deteriorated backward psychotic people were at one time at least marginally adjusted.

In systems terms we can make the point most emphatically. There is no such thing as a level of dysfunction in the misadventure of schizophrenia. And there is not a level of causation—not even if we demonstrate a genetic or constitutional inheritance.

Epilogue: Some Comments on the Treatment of Schizophrenia

In my view the classical triad of hospitalization, drugs and family reaffiliation will usually ameliorate the psychosis but sustain the schizophrenic condition. I believe that hospitalization and drugs alone—without a program of rehabilitation and the development of personal relationships—will ultimately foster a chronic psychotic state.

It is also my personal conviction that an adequate individual psychotherapy can terminate psychosis, prevent psychotic episodes and produce an improvement in schizophrenia, but I think certain conditions must be met for this to happen. The therapy must be intensive and active. I do not think a purely free associative therapy with guidance and interaction is adequate. In fact, I think a psychotherapy which relies upon insight alone can be risky, for it can foster failures and even psychotic episodes. The basis for my opinion is this. A purely uncovering type of therapy focuses upon the patient's defenses, i.e., upon his withdrawal from relationships and life experiences. Such a therapy can encourage the patient to attempt courtship, education and employment. *But in the absence of coaching, identifications and other methods of inducing more interactional experience and linear abilities, I think such encouragement may lead to further failures and hence to further withdrawals.*

For this reason, I think it is imperative that we develop methods to teach interactional skills and linear abilities. To be sure, such teaching is implicit in many therapies and rehabilitation procedures, *but I think these approaches must be conscious, purposeful and much improved.* We must learn to develop them and employ them directly and rapidly in all instances of schizophrenia before and between psychotic episodes. I should be more specific. I think we must extend the principles of vocational rehabilitation. We must not only teach physical tasks but interactional ones as well. We must teach appropriate tactile, gaze and orientation behavior. We must teach territorial behavior, for example, the rules of occupying space and respecting the spaces of other people. And we must teach the principles of narration and exposition.

Some therapies now teach methods of interpersonal confrontation, but I think this is not likely to be successful with schizophrenic people until they are more accomplished in the more basic behavior of interaction. In addition, I do not think that confrontational behavior should be taught without also teaching the behavior of coaction, i.e., of alliance and cooperation. When we have taught schizophrenic people about occupying spaces, forming orientations, taking appropriate distances and making contact, then we can consider the teaching of specific forms of interactions—forms such as confrontation, conversation and courtship.

One must raise a practical objection. Many schizophrenic people are terrified about interpersonal accomplishments. It is ridiculous to attempt to teach someone to accomplish the very things he dreads. Some schizophrenic people, however, are most eager to learn such things, and those who fear to do so can be encouraged by insight therapies. In short, one can combine therapeutic work about over-loyalty to a symbiotic partner and fears of relating with the actual teaching of communicative skills.

There is also a theoretical objection to such procedures. It is possible that one who has not learned such skills in growing up lacks the neural development to accomplish them later. We cannot now answer this question, but I think it is imperative that we find out. We will not find out, though, until we have developed the intent and the teaching skills and tried them exhaustively on a large number of schizophrenic people.

Personally, I have never seen a schizophrenic person who could not learn something about touch, gaze, narration and the formation of relationships. Sometimes the results are striking. To my knowledge reports of efforts to teach communication behaviors to schizophrenics have not yet been published, but one impressive example has been presented at a public meeting (Yorberg et al., 1978). In this study, mothers and autistic children were required to hold and look at each other several hours each day. Within weeks there was a dramatic improvement in each instance of behavior and in the ability to write, read and speak.

It is probable that in the near future we will have a threefold approach to the treatment of schizophrenic psychosis. We will have improved and less dangerous medications, ways of reestablishing social affiliation, and methods of insight therapy which are combined with education towards maturity.

There is an aspect of these issues which may be even more important than treatment. We must someday learn how to prevent the development of schizophrenia. The view I have taken, the view of a series of escalating vicious cycles, makes it possible that the interruption of any of these at any age might help to prevent the relentless amplification of deviance which accrues as the child gets older. In this case earlier and earlier recognition of the deficiencies is important. But to carry this notion to its ultimate conclusion brings us to the hope of preventing the schizophrenic problem in the early weeks of life. *If an infant is deficient in alertness and contact, we should be able to help a mother recognize this immediately, and then we can help her find ways to make an extra effort.* If the mother or other family members have difficulty in making contact with an infant, we must help them learn how to do so, just as we now prepare a young couple for parenthood in other dimensions of baby care. It is my dream that we will learn how to do this.

References

ANGYAL, A.: Disturbances of thinking in schizophrenia. In *Language and Thought in Schizophrenia*, edited by Kasanin, J. S., Univ. of Ca. Press, Los Angeles, 1951.

ARIETI, S.: *Interpretation of Schizophrenia*. Robert Brunner, New York, 1955.

ARIETI, S.: *Interpretation of Schizophrenia*. Basic Books, New York, Second Edition, 1974.

BATESON, G.: *Steps to an Ecology of Mind*. Ballantine Books, New York, 1972.

BATESON, G., JACKSON, D. D., HALEY, J., and WEAKLAND, J.: Toward a theory of schizophrenia. *Behavioral Sci.*, 1: 251-264, 1956.

BEAUMONT, J. G., and DIAMOND, S. J.: Brain disconnection and schizophrenia. *Br. J. Psychiatry*, 123: 661-662, 1973.

BENEDICT, R.: *Patterns of Culture*. Mentor, New York, 1946.

BIRD, E.: Paper at Collegium, International Neuro-Psychopharmacologicum, 1978.

BIRDWHISTELL, R. L.: *Kinesics and Context*. University of Pennsylvania Press, Philadelphia, 1970.

BLAU, T. H.: Torque and schizophrenic vulnerability. *Amer. Psychologist*, 32:12, 997-1005, 1977.

BLEULER, E.: *Dementia Praecox or the Group of Schizophrenias*. J. Zinkin (transl.). Int'l Univ. Press, New York, 1950.

BOWEN, M.: A family concept of schizophrenia. In *The Etiology of Schizophrenia*. Edited by Jackson, D. D., Basic Books, New York, 1960.

BOWEN, M.: The use of family theory in clinical practice. *Comprehensive Psychiatry*, 7: 345-374, 1966.

BOWEN, M.: Observed on a videotape made by Milton Berger at the Beyond the Double Bind Conference, New York, 1977.

BOWEN, M.: *Family Therapy in Clinical Practice*. Jason Aronson, New York, 1978. (a)

BOWEN, M.: Schizophrenia as a multi-generational phenomenon. In *Beyond the Double Bind*. Edited by Berger, M. M., Brunner/Mazel, New York, 1978. (b)

BYCHOWSKI, G.: *Psychotherapy of Psychoses*. Grune & Stratton, New York, 1952.

CARLSSON, A.: Antipsychotic drugs, neurotransmitters and schizophrenia. *Amer. J. Psychiat.*, 135: 2, 164-173, (Feb.), 1978.

CHAPMAN, L. J. and CHAPMAN, J. P.: *Disordered Thought in Schizophrenia*. Prentice-Hall, Englewood Cliffs, N.J., 1973.

CONDON, W. S.: Multiple response to sound dysfunctional children. *J. Autism and Child Schiz.*, 5: 37, 1975.

CRIDER, A.: *Schizophrenia: A Biopsychological Perspective*. Halsted Press, New York, 1979.

CROW, T., and OWEN, F.: Paper at Collegium, International Neuro-Psychopharmacologicum, 1978.

DUHL, F.: Personal communication, 1978.

EFRON, D.: *Gesture and Environment*. King's Crown, New York, 1941.

ENGLISH, O. S.: Personal communication, 1962.

ERIKSON, K.: *Wayward Puritans: A Study of the Sociology of Deviance.* Wiley, New York, 1966.

FARLEY, I. J., PRICE, K. S., and McCULLOUGH, E.: Norepinephrine in chronic paranoid schizophrenia. *Science,* 200: 456-457, 1978.

FEDERN, P.: *Ego Psychology and the Psychoses.* Basic Books, New York, 1952.

FERBER, J.: Personal communication, 1978.

FLOR, H. P.: Schizophrenic-like reactions and affective psychoses associated with temporal lobe epilepsy. *Amer. J. Psychiat.,* 126: 400-404, 1969.

FOUCAULT, M.: *Madness and Civilization.* Random House, New York, 1965.

FREUD, A.: *The Ego and the Mechanisms of Defense.* Int. Univ. Press, New York, 1946.

FREUD, S.: A case of dementia paranoidis. *Collected Papers,* Vol. III. Hogarth Press, London, 1949.

FROMM-REICHMANN, F.: *Principles of Intensive Psychotherapy,* University of Chicago Press, Chicago, 1950.

GOFFMAN, E.: *Asylums.* Doubleday, Garden City, New York, 1961.

GOLDSTEIN, K.: Methodological approach to the study of schizophrenic thought disorder. In *Language and Thought in Schizophrenia.* Edited by Kasanin, J. S., Univ. of Ca. Press, Los Angeles, 1951.

GUNDERSON, J. G., AUTRY, J. H., III, MOSHER, L. R. et al.: Special Report: Schizophrenia. *Schizophrenia Bull.* (NIMH), Washington, D.C. 9:16-54, 1974.

GUR, R. E.: Left hemisphere dysfunction and left hemisphere overactivation in schizophrenia. *J. Abnorm. Psychol.,* 87:226-238, 1978.

HARROW, M., HIMMELHOCH, J., TUCKER, G., HERSH, J., and QUINLAN, D.: Overinclusive thinking in acute schizophrenic patients. *J. Abnorm. Psychol.,* 79: 2, 161-163, 1972.

HOBSON, J. A., and McCARLEY, R. W.: The brain as a dream state generator: An activation-synthesis hypothesis of the dream process. *Amer. J. Psychiat.,* 134: 1335-1348, 1977.

JASPERS, K.: *General Psychopathology.* The University of Chicago Press, Chicago, 1963.

JAYNES, J.: *The Origins of Consciousness in the Breakdown of the Bicameral Mind.* Houghton-Mifflin, Boston, 1976.

KENDON, A.: *Studies in the Behavior of Social Interaction.* Humanities Press, Atlantic Highlands, N.J., 1977.

KENDON, A., and FERBER, A.: A description of some behavior greetings. In *Comparative Ecology and Behavior of Primates.* Edited by Michael, R. P., and Cook, J. H., Academic Press, London, 1975.

KERNBERG, O.: Borderline personality organizations. *J. Amer. Psychoanal. Assn.,* 15: 641-685, 1968.

KETY, S. S., ROSENTHAL, D., WENDER, P. H., and SCHULSINGER, F.: Mental illness in the biological and adoptive families of adopted schizophrenics. *Amer. J. Psychiat.,* 128: 302-306, 1971.

KINSBOURNE, M.: The mechanism of hemispheric control of the lateral gradient of attention. In *Attention and Performance,* V. Edited by Rabbitt, P. M. A., and Dornic, S., Academic Press, London, 1975.

KLEIN, M.: *Contributions to Psychoanalysis.* Hogarth Press, London, 1948.

KOFFKA, K.: *Principles of Gestalt Psychology.* Harcourt, New York, 1935.

KRAEPELIN, E.: *Lectures on Clinical Psychiatry.* Bailliere, Tindall & Cox, London, 1906. (Thos. Johnson, transl.)

KUHN, T. S.: *The Structure of Scientific Revolutions.* Univ. of Chicago Press, Chicago, 1962.

LEATON, R. N.: The limbic system and its psychopharmacological aspects. In *An Introduction to Psychopharmacology,* Edited by Rich, R. H. and Moore, K. E., Raven, New York, 1975.

LEWIN, K.: *Field Theory in Social Science.* Edited by Cartwright, B., Harper Bros., New York, 1951.

LEWIS, N. D. C.: *Research in Dementia Praecox.* Nat. Comm. Ment. Hyg., New York, 1936.

LIDZ, T.: *The Origins and Treatment of Schizophrenic Disorders.* Basic Books, New York, 1973.

MAHLER, M. S.: On child psychosis and schizophrenia. *Psychoanal. Study of the Child.* Vol. VII. Int'l Univ. Press, New York, 1952.

MAHLER, M. S.: Autism and symbiosis. *Int. J. Psychoanalysis,* 39: 77-83, 1958.

MAHLER, M. S.: Certain aspects of the separation-individuation phase. *Psychoanal. Quart.,* 29: 317-327, 1963.

MAHLER, M. S. and LA PERRIERE, K.: Mother-child interaction during separation-individuation. *Psychoanal. Quart.,* 34: 483-498, 1965.

MASSE, H.: Personal communication, 1973.

McQUOWN, N. A., et al.: *The Natural History of the Interview.* Microfilm collection of manuscripts in cultural anthropology. Series XV. #95, 96, 97, 98. Univ. of Chicago Library, 1971.

MEAD, G. H.: *Mind, Self and Society.* Univ. of Chicago Press, Chicago, 1934.

MEDNICK, S. and SCHULSINGER, F.: Studies of children at high risk for schizophrenia. Presented at the 1970 Dean Award Ceremony in San Diego, California, January, 1972.

MILLER, G. A., GALANTER, E., and PRIBRAM, K. H.: *Plans and the Structure of Behavior.* Holt & Co., New York, 1960.

ORNSTEIN, R. E.: *The Psychology of Consciousness* (2nd ed.). Harcourt, New York, 1977.

PALAZZOLI, M. S., BOSCOLO, L., CECCHIN, G., and PRATA, G.: *Paradox and Counterparadox.* Jason Aronson, New York, 1978.

PAULING, L.: Orthomolecular psychiatry. *Science,* 160: 265-271, 1968.

PAVLOV, I. P.: *Lectures on Conditioned Reflexes.* St. Martin's Press, New York, 1979. (Reprint of 1927 Edition).

PENFIELD, W.: Consciousness, memory and man's conditioned reflexes. In *On the Biology of Learning.* Edited by Pribram, K. H., Harcourt, New York, 1969.

PRIBRAM, K. H.: *Languages of the Brain.* Prentice-Hall, Englewood Cliffs, N.J., 1971.

ROSEN, J. N.: *Direct Analysis.* Grune and Stratton, New York, 1953.

ROSENTHAL, R.: *Experiment Effects on Behavioral Research.* Halsted Press, New York, 1976.

SAPIR, E.: *Language.* Harcourt, New York, 1921.

SCHEFLEN, A. E.: *A Psychotherapy of Schizophrenia: Direct Analysis.* Charles C Thomas, Springfield, Ill., 1960. (a)

SCHEFLEN, A. E.: Regressive one-to-one relationships, *Psychiat. Quart,* 34: 692 (Oct), 1960. (b)

SCHEFLEN, A. E.: Communication and regulation in psychotherapy. *Psychiatry,* 26: 126, May, 1963.

SCHEFLEN, A. E.: *Body Language and Social Order,* Prentice-Hall, Englewood Cliffs, N.J., 1972.

SCHEFLEN, A. E.: *Communicational Structure,* Indiana University Press, Bloomington, 1973.

SCHEFLEN, A. E.: *How Behavior Means.* Doubleday, Garden City, N.Y., 1974.

SCHEFLEN, A. E.: On teaching communicative skills. In *Rehabilitation Medicine and Psychiatry.* Edited by Meislin, J., Charles C Thomas, Springfield, Ill., 1976.

SCHEFLEN, A. E.: Double-bind theory and schizophrenia. In *Beyond the Double Bind.* Edited by Berger, M. M., Brunner/Mazel, New York, 1978.

SCHNEIDER, K.: *Clinical Psychopathology,* Grune and Stratton, New York, 1959.

SEARLES, H. F.: Dependency processes in the psychotherapy of schizophrenia. *J. Amer. Psychoanal Assn.*, 3: 19-36, 1955.

SHAKOW, D.: Segmental set: The adaptive process in schizophrenia. *Archives of General Psychiatry*, 6: 1-17, 1962.

SINGER, M. C., WYNNE, L. C., and TOOHEY, M. I.: Communication disorders and the families of schizophrenics. In *Nature of Schizophrenia*. Edited by Wynne, L. C., Cromwell, R. L., and Matthysse, S., Wiley, New York, 1978.

SPITZ, R. A.: Hospitalism. *Psychoanal. Study of the Child*, Vol. II. Int. Univ. Press, New York, 1946.

STERN, D. N.: A micro-analysis of the mother-infant interaction. *J. Child Psychiat.*, 10: 501 (July) 1974.

SUGERMAN, A. A., GOLDSTEIN, L., MARJERRISON, G., and STOLTZFUSS, N.: Recent research in EEG amplitude analysis. Presented at the 5th World Congress of Psychiatry, Mexico City, 1971.

SULLIVAN, H. S.: *The Interpersonal Theory of Psychiatry*. Norton, New York, 1953.

SULLIVAN, H. S.: Therapeutic investigation in schizophrenia. *Psychiatry*, 10:121, 1947.

SZASZ, T.: *Law, Liberty and Psychiatry*. Macmillan, New York, 1963.

TACHETOMA, F.: Personal communication, 1977.

TOLMAN, E. C.: Cognitive maps in rats and men. *Psychol. Rev.*, 55: 217-289, 1948.

URSTAD, H.: Hemispheric dominance: A temporal lobe shift in psychotic behavior. *J. of the Oslo City Hospitals*, 1979.

VON BERTALANFFY, L.: *General Systems Theory: Foundations, Development, Applications*. Braziller, New York, 1968.

VON DOMARUS, E.: The specific laws of logic in schizophrenia. In *Language and Thought in Schizophrenia*. Edited by Kasanin, J. S., Univ. of Ca. Press, Los Angeles, 1951.

WEINER, N.: *Cybernetics*. Wiley, New York, 1948.

WERTHEIMER, M.: *Drei Abhandlungen Zür Gestalttheorie*, Erlangen Philosophische Akademie, 1925.

WEXLER, B. E.: Cerebral laterality and psychiatry: A review of the literature. *Am. J. Psychiat.*, 137: 3, 279-291, 1980.

WINNICOTT, D. W.: Transitional objects and transitional phenomena. *Int. J. Psychoanal.*, 34: 483-498, 1953.

WRIGHT, S.: Personal communication, 1965.

WYNNE, L. C.: Communication disorders and the quest for relatedness in families of schizophrenics. *Amer. J. of Psychoanal.*, 30: 2, 100-114, 1970.

WYNNE, L. C., RYCKOFF, I. M., DAY, J., and HIRSH, S. I.: Pseudomutuality in the family relations of schizophrenia, *Psychiatry*, 22: 205, 1958.

WYNNE, L. C., SINGER, M. T., BARTKO, J. J., and TOOHEY, M. L.: Schizophrenics and their families. In *Developments in Psychiatric Research*. Edited by Tanner, J. M., Hoddon and Stroughton, London, 1977.

YORBERG, L., WELSH, M., FERBER, J., FERBER, A., SCHANE, M., and SCHEFLEN, A. E.: Forced hugging therapy for autistic children. Presented at American Orthopsychiatric Assoc. Meeting, San Francisco, March, 1978.

Index